APPARITIONS IN
Betania
Venezuela

MARY, VIRGIN AND MOTHER OF
RECONCILIATION OF ALL PEOPLE

Sister Margaret Catherine Sims, CSJ

MEDUGORJE-MESSENGERS
P. O. Box 647
Framingham, MA 01701
Tel. (508) 879-9318
FAX (508) 879-9303

"I thank my God every time I remember you."

(Phillipians 1:3)

Acknowledgements:

Maria Esperanza de Bianchini for being *you.*

Bishop Pio Bello Ricardo and Rev. Otty Ossa Aristizabal for permission to translate and print some of the material used in this book.

My Community, the Sisters of Saint Joseph of Boston, who have always supported me as I have tried to follow where the Spirit led.

Medugorje Messengers Staff, Volunteers, and Pilgrims for their support and encouragement.

Sister Malcolm Galvin, CSJ, for translating Father Otty's Book from Spanish into English and Sister Annette Daly, CSJ, (deceased) for typing it.

Sister Frances Scribner, smsm, friend, *"journey"* companion, and editor of this book.

© Copyright 1992 by Sister Margaret Catherine Sims, CSJ
All rights reserved.
Published by Medugorje Messengers
P.O. Box 647, Framingham, MA 01701

Library of Congress Catalog Card Number: 93–80482
ISBN #: 0-9639504-9-5

Second Printing November, 1993

Printed By
STAR LITHO, INC.
2 Powerhouse Road
South Boston, Massachusetts 02127
U.S.A.

Author's Note

Called by Our Lady to write this book about her apparitions in Betania, Venezuela, I did not give any consideration to the financing of it until the manuscript was in the hands of the printer. How would I pay for it?

The printer received the manuscript on May 7th, and the following day I called "Jack" and explained my predicament to him. Just the day before, Jack had said to Our Lady in prayer, "Mary, my Mother, I really want to serve you in a special way." Jack then said to me, "Sister Margaret, Our Lady called you to write her book and she has asked me to finance it." Jack knew before I told him how much it was going to cost.

I was called by Our Lady to write this book; Jack was called to finance it and *you* are being called to read it and to live the messages of "Mary, Virgin and Mother of Reconciliation of All People."

TABLE OF CONTENTS

Introduction

INTRODUCTION

Around noon on December 20th, 1989 I heard the name Betania for the first time, and my initial reaction was very similar to hearing the word Medugorje for the first time. I wanted to go to Betania as soon as possible to check out the apparitions. I had several questions and wanted to find some answers.

Who? When? Where? What? These were just a few of the questions.

After calling a Travel Agency and making arrangements to fly to Venezeula on January 3rd, 1990, I called a friend, Sister Frances Scribner, smsm, and asked, "Sister Frances how you would like to be my companion to Venezuela?" "Where?" "Venezuela."

Sister Frances eventually agreed to ask her Provincial for the permission to accompany me to Betania. However, I have always suspected that at the time, she was praying that the answer would be no.

We left J.F.K. Airport on January 3rd and although we were slated to arrive in Caracas around 9:00 p.m. the plane was delayed leaving New York and we didn't arrive until 11:30 p.m.

Neither of us was fluent in Spanish and we had no idea where our hotel was or how we were going to get there at this time of night.

The Holy Spirit was with us and Our Lady was guiding us because after collecting our luggage and going through Customs, we walked outside the airport and hailed a taxi. A car with no exterior markings of a taxi pulled up and for the first time we met "Jose." Jose became our chaffeur and guide for the rest of the trip. He didn't speak English, but with the help of a dictionary and a little Spanish, all went well during the week.

Our week-long stay in Caracas and particularly Betania was filled with graces and blessings, and this book is an attempt to make others aware of the apparitions in Betania, Venezuela where Our Lady appears as "Mary, Virgin and Mother of Reconciliation of All People."

To my mothers:

Catherine, you gave me life

Margaret, you nurtured that life

Mary, my Mother, you brought me life - your Son, Jesus.

Chapter 1

What Does The Catholic Church Say About The Apparitions?

1

What Does The Catholic Church Say About The Apparitions In Betania?

Betania is one of the four approved apparitions of the 20th century. The quotation below is an excerpt from a Pastoral Letter issued by Bishop Pio Bello Ricardo, the bishop of the diocese of Los Teques in the State of Miranda, Venezuela. It is the diocese where Betania is located.

"From the beginning of my investigation, I noticed that it was not a case of fraud, collective suggestion or promotion of people or group interests but rather it dealt with a serious subject which had to be seriously investigated.

"Relatively soon, along with my investigation, I became certain about the supernatural character of the phenomenon. I decided however to follow prudent practice and postpone all explicit statements about the phenomenon. With subsequent statements I would gauge the effects obtained and make critical pursuit of the religious movement produced by the events. I would then judge the opportune moment at hand for making public my judgement on these events.

"Consequently, after having studied repeatedly the apparitions of the most Holy Virgin Mary in Betania, and having begged the Lord earnestly for spiritual discernment, *I declare that in my judgement, said apparitions are authentic and have a supernatural character.*

"I approve, therefore, officially, that the site where the same have occurred be considered as sacred, and that the same be kept as a place for pilgrimages and as a place for prayer, reflection and worship in that the liturgical acts may be performed, especially the celebration of the Mass and the administration of the sacraments of Reconciliation and the Eucharist, always in accordance with the laws of the Church and the norms of the diocese and pastoral unity."

Chapter 2

Where Is Betania?

2

Where is Betania?

To get to Betania it is necessary to fly to Caracas, Venezuela, which is about a three hour flight from Miami, Florida and six hours from Boston, Massachusetts. It is possible to fly to Caracas from almost any large city in the United States.

Betania is an agricultural area located in the diocese of Los Teques in the State of Miranda, Venezuela. The site of the apparitions is a very simple "finca" or farm. A large outdoor altar with a tin roof provides shelter from the sun or rain for about four hundred people. Behind the altar there is a grotto carved out of the rocks with a beautiful statue of Our Lady of Lourdes nestled within.

The grotto is usually surrounded with beautiful flowers and hundreds of votive candles. To the right of the grotto is a cascade of water from a mountain spring. Many people have claimed to have been healed after drinking water from the cascade.

Picnic tables can be found on the grounds, but there are no food stands so it is necessary to bring your own provisions. Restrooms are available on the grounds.

The atmosphere at Betania is very peaceful and very prayerful during the week. On weekends thousands of people flock to Betania and it is still a very prayerful place. But with many Masses, processions, songs and rosaries, it might be a little difficult to find a "quiet" place to pray.

It is interesting to note that "Betania" translates into Bethany, a favorite spot of Jesus and His Mother.

It was there that they visited so often with their friends, Martha and Mary, and their brother, Lazarus, and enjoyed fellowship and relaxation.

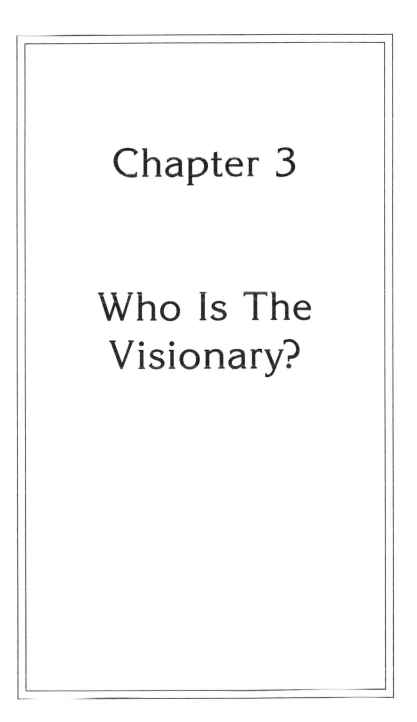

Chapter 3

Who Is The Visionary?

3

Who Is The Visionary?

The principal visionary of the apparitions in Betania is Maria Esperanza de Bianchini. She was born on November 22nd, 1928 in the town of Barrancas, a part of the State of Monagas, Venezuela.

Her father Aniceto Medrano died when Maria Esperanza was two years old leaving her mother Maria Filomena Parra de Medrano the task of raising Maria and her four brothers. Her mother worked very hard trying to provide materially for her children, but always, she was interested in teaching and training her children strong Christian values and impressing upon them the importance of the spiritual life. Her daily life was an example in spirituality for them.

Maria listened to her mother's teaching and at a very early age was praying to God and the saints. One day at the age of five, Maria Esperanza was saying goodbye to her mother who was going on a trip. At that moment, feeling very sad, Maria felt a force impelling her to look towards the river. There standing at the Port of Bolivar City she saw St. Theresa of the Little Flower emerging from the waters of the Orinoco River. St. Theresa threw a rose to her. Maria went running to her mother with the rose in her hand.

When Maria was ten years old her family moved to Caracas, Venezuela. Two years later she became very sick with bronchial pneumonia and it was during this sickness that Our Lady appeared to Maria for the first time.

At the age of fourteen Maria was ill again due this time to problems with her heart. One day Maria felt herself at the brink of death. She beseeched the Sacred Heart of Jesus to either heal her or allow her to rest in peace. At once she saw the Image of the Sacred Heart of Jesus. He told her: "Maria Esperanza, my Mother and I will heal you. Do not despair, you will find peace and relief of your sufferings. My Father has heard you and you will rise."

Maria Esperanza was healed at that moment much to the amazement of her doctors.

Most of her life Maria Esperanza had dreamed of entering a religious community and becoming a nun. She even entered the Franciscan Sisters of Merida, in Los Andes. However on October 3rd, 1954, St. Theresa, the Little Flower, appeared to Maria Esperanza while she was praying with the nuns in the chapel. For the second time St. Theresa threw a rose to her. Maria tried to catch it but felt it pinch and leave a drop of blood in her hand. St. Theresa told her that Our Lord was calling her to the world. Her vocation was not to become a nun but rather a wife and mother. After this Maria saw Our Lord who gave her a message telling her that she had to go to Rome to receive the blessings of the Holy Father. Here she would find her truth.

Shortly after leaving the convent Maria Esperanza met her future husband Geo Bianchini Giani and they were married on December 8th, 1956 in the Chapel of the Immaculate Conception in St. Peter's

Basilica, Rome, Italy. It was the first marriage to take place in this chapel. They have seven children, six daughters and one son.

For many years Our Lady had been preparing Maria Esperanza for what would eventually take place in Betania. She revealed to her that Betania would be a special haven of prayer and refuge for all her children. She described the place to Maria in detail. There would be many trees, majestic and beautiful. There would be a river in front of humble dwellings and there would be a grotto with a fountain of threads of water which would spring up and flow unceasingly.

Our Lady promised Maria Esperanza that when this place was found she would appear to her there and afterwards she would be visible to many who came there to pray.

Maria and her husband Geo spent much prayer and time trying to find a place that would resemble Our Lady's plan for a place of prayer and worship. Finally, in March 1974, with the help of two other families, Mr. and Mrs. Jesus Andreu and Mr. and Mrs. Jose Castellano, Maria and Geo Bianchini purchased the land now known as Betania.

What a blessing that day was for all of them because what had been a dream for so many years was now on the way to becoming a reality.

It was a time of great work for them, but also a time of great joy. They spent most of their free time clearing and preparing the area so that people could come to Betania to relax and to pray.

Maria and Geo returned to Rome with their children and spent most of 1975 and the beginning of 1976 there taking care of Geo's mother who was old and infirm.

After returning to Venezuela in 1976, they soon found themselves spending as much time as possible in Betania especially on the weekends. The first apparition occurred on March 25th, 1976, the feast of the Annunciation. The only one to see Mary that day was Maria Esperanza. Many of her friends and relatives had accompanied Maria to Betania. Although they did not see Our Lady, they did witness other phenomena: a pulsating of the sun, a mist covering the mountain, a profusion of flowers where none existed, singing from an invisible choir and a brilliant light.

On Sunday March 25th, 1984 approximately one hundred and fifty people gathered for the celebration of Mass at noon. After Mass most of the group wandered around the area talking, eating and sharing with each other.

Meanwhile, some youths stayed to play near the waterfall and they were startled to see Our Lady appearing behind it. They ran to spread the news of the apparition and all hastened to the site. While they were talking about Our Lady appearing there was another apparition and all present saw the Blessed Mother.

During the afternoon there occurred seven apparitions in all. Most of the apparitions lasted five or ten minutes, except the last apparition at dusk, which lasted approximately one half hour.

Maria Esperanza de Bianchini spends most weekends and Holy Days at Betania and Our Lady continues to appear to her. Like Padre Pio, Maria Esperanza has had, and continues to have many mystical experiences. Every Good Friday she suffers with the stigmata. People have been healed through her intercessory prayers. At times the Eucharist mysteriously appears on her tongue. The aroma of roses, as well as other sweet smelling flowers, is evident in her presence. Recently rose buds and a rose have appeared on her chest.

Although blessed with so many spiritual gifts, Maria Esperanza has remained a very humble, loving, caring mother to her own children and to all her "spiritual" children who visit Betania.

Chapter 4

What Happened In Betania?

4

What Happened In Betania?

OFFICIAL STATEMENT OF MARIA ESPERANZA DE BIANCHINI

In the name of the Father, of the Son and of the Holy Spirit, Amen.

I think obedience is the small particle of gold that is building, so quickly and with spiritual joy, the soul of a child of God who is learning to practice the magnificent lessons that her Master teaches her. Oh, may I be obedient in all things.

I am well disposed to speak and to write about the events which have taken place pertaining to the apparitions at Betania where Our Lady, Mother and Reconciler of All People, visits us.

It is by request, or better yet, command of his Exellency Bishop Pio Bello Ricardo that I attempt to describe what happened at Betania on March 25th, 1976 when Our Lady appeared to me there for the first time.

Yes, Our Lady had been preparing me for many years since I was fourteen when she would say to me: "In the course of time you will buy a house and that property will have a river which will pass in front of

19

the house. In the middle of the woods with thick verdure, among beautiful fruit trees of bananas, sugar cane, mangos, water chestnuts, tangerines, avocadoes and guave trees I will be present. That place will also have a rocky grotto with threads of water which will spring up unceasingly and it will be surrounded with large leafy majestic trees, and in this place I shall appear to you and then afterwards I shall be visible to others."

The years passed and on March 31st, 1974 the "Promised Land" became a reality for us. Together with two other couples, dear friends of ours, we signed the document of ownership on June 28th, 1974.

Because "Nona", my husband's mother, was sick it was necessary for our entire family to go to Rome to be with her. Although we missed going to Betania, it was a time of much happiness to be together in Rome for the Holy Year.

At the beginning of 1976 Our Heavenly Mother touched my soul in a very gentle manner telling me that it would soon be time to return to Caracas. On February 9th, 1976, Our Blessed Mother under the title of Our Lady of Lourdes ordered me to return to Caracas some time between the middle and end of the month because my presence was necessary there. I felt a great deal of pain and suffering at having to leave my family for even a few days. It was now very clear to me that Our Lady's apparitions in this chosen place were near, so I returned to Caracas.

In Caracas on March 11th, 21st and 24th I was being asked to submit to a test, and, although I was

20

surrounded by affection and considerate people, I still felt very much alone.

During those days my Mother commanded me to spend the time in seclusion and silence. It was a time of prayer, meditation and penance. My food was only barley and fruit juices as I was preparing to experience and live a few moments in her presence. On the 25th of March she would be visible to me.

At 8:30 a.m. on March 25th, 1976 she appeared to me through the branches of a big tree at Betania. I saw a large cloud that came out of the interior and hovered over the top of the tree. It was an immense cloud-like smoke, and someone said, "Look, Maria, look at the smoke; the house is burning." I stared at the cloud and the cloud seemed to open and out came the Holy Virgin.

I saw Mary all dressed in white with a most beautiful face, a rosy light brown color, very beautiful and delicate, with brown eyes, well defined eyebrows, and a small mouth with an ineffable sweetness. Her hair which was dark chestnut fell over her shoulders. I shall never forget her eyes; even now they are engraved in my being. They were gentle eyes that looked at me tenderly as if inviting me to live a life worthy of experiencing her presence and of looking upon her continually.

She was a ray of light that penetrated my soul, shaking all the fibers of my heart in the total depths of my being. Interiorly I felt so humble, so weak, so incapable; I was nothing compared to this beauty that was dazzling me. Her whole being continued to radiate light and my whole body began to tremble.

21

The shouts of the others brought me back to reality and I witnessed the sun whirling with all its colors in the sky.

Again, Our Lady's face was so delicate and young as a child of approximately fourteen to sixteen years old. Her attire was very soft and white and bright. It really showed off a very beautiful image of my Mother. She appeared to be wearing a white mantle over her shoulders and on her head she had some kind of a veil that became tangled in the trees. From her hands, which were open and stretched out about waist level, came rays in all directions. It was as if she were inviting me to approach her. I wanted to fly to her and be cradled in her breast.

Then Mary opened her lips and she said to me, "Little daughter, you are beholding me with my hands outstretched with graces and wrapped in the splendor of light to call all my children to conversion; this is the seed of glory that I offer as Virgin Mother and Mother, Reconciler of People, because I come to reconcile them. Reconciliation is the inheritance of the divine fraternity of my Divine Son. Little daughter bring my message to all. I shall keep you here in my heart from this day onward."

I saw shining sparks of light falling over everyone. There were enormous quantities of the falling sparks, so much so, that when it was over, I was covered with a golden frost. Inwardly I continued to experience the presence of my heavenly Mother inviting me to surrender to the Lord and to adore, praise and love Him silently. I was able to surrender with confidence and to make the resolution to listen to the Lord and to accept and do His will. "Oh Mother, Mary how good you have been to me! It was wonderful!"

There were about eighty people with me, but they did not see Our Lady. She had told me in a message earlier that morning that she would come, but only I would see her.

Father Laborem and Father Molina came looking for me because earlier I had informed Bishop Bernal, the bishop of Los Teques at the time, that the Virgin was going to appear to me. He said, "Good, Maria Esperanza, but you know that when events occur such as, her looking at you or speaking to you, there will be a great responsibility placed on you with much suffering and you must be brave."

Bishop Bernal comforted me and said, "Maria, I know it is the truth. I have followed your life and I know that God wants something special and beautiful from you. Don't ever forget, my daughter, He will ask much of you, but He will give much to you." He then told me that these two priests would be coming and that they would celebrate Mass that day. It was beautiful! Many people came to receive the sacraments of Reconciliation and Holy Eucharist. It was very beneficial for all.

I want to make it clear that I did not tell the people that came with me to Betania that Our Lady would appear to me, but I indicated to them when she was leaving and that we would see colors and the sun spinning. I was afraid to say that I was going to see Our Lady, for I wasn't sure if they we're going to see her as well, but they realized I was seeing her the moment she appeared.

They asked me many questions about the apparition, but I told them I could not speak about it yet, but that soon I would be able to and then we would all feel Our Lady's presence. Then I told them, "In 1977 and in 1978 she will appear again; however very few will see her."

For me that day in March, 1976 was a day that I shall never forget. The expression on her face moved me; her eyes were so gentle yet they pierced the very depths of my being. There was something so special about this apparition that, even though many apparitions were to follow, this one had placed a seal and I would be in her arms always no matter what would happen in my life.

Time passed and I had to return to Rome. On the 2nd of May I received a message from the Virgin as Mary, Queen and Mother in which she told me to prepare myself in a special manner because a light would illuminate my soul before August.

With God's help and the help of my most Holy Mother my whole family had the opportunity to take a vacation so that at the end of July we were all in Caracas.

About two weeks before the 22nd of August she asked me to erect a cross at the entrance to the apparition site. On August 22nd she appeared to me again clothed in white with her heart shining brightly. She smiled at me. She was wearing a blue sash at her waist as she did at Lourdes. As she smiled at me I felt very touched and wept copiously. I could not hold back the tears. She seemed so close to me and I heard her murmur, "Little daughter, when all people of the earth take up their cross lovingly, then there will be no more pain, nor weeping, nor death, because they will live rising each day with my most beloved Son in a constant and living ALLELUIA! ALLELUIA! ALLELUIA!"

She also said, "My little daughter, I want you to help them realize the value of prayer and the importance of my recent apparition as Reconciler of People. It is under this title that you will encounter the essential and definite conditions to receive the grace of the Holy Spirit. Prepare your souls to receive these graces by praying for faith. Little daughter, faith is the foundation of the Christian and an increase of faith will bring you to seek with sincere love, our Father and the heart of my Divine Son joined with mine."

It was very touching for me to see so many people including Don Simon Adreu and his wife Berta approaching me with outstretched arms and tears rolling down their cheeks. They were remembering their son Simonette who used to accompany my son Jesus to Betania, but he had died recently. That day all who were present signed a book that I keep giving testimony of a great day of light and hope for all reaffirming therefore the presence of Mary Our Heavenly Mother among us.

On March 25th, 1977, the Virgin appeared to me again and this time there were about fifteen people present. The rays of the sun dazzled us and fell on the branches of a big tree. It was a beautiful day and the atmosphere was permeated with the sweet fragrance of roses, lilies and spikenard. I could sense

St. Joseph was telling me, "I shall watch over this 'Fountain of Love' with Jesus and Mary so that this town may be saved, because the family is the hope of the new world."

On the 27th of November in 1977, the Virgin Mary appeared to me again. It was the feast of the Miraculous Medal. She said that she would appear to me again on the 25th of March, 1978 and that the group who would accompany me to Betania would also have the opportunity to experience her presence and to see her.

On the 8th of December 1977, I was with a group of relatives and friends when we brought a statue of Our Lady of Lourdes and St. Bernadette to the grotto. As we were approaching the grotto singing and praying we could see a blue butterfly above our heads and two smaller ones. These butterflies continued to follow us. A friend of mine, Noris Behrens, said to me, "Maria Esperanza, do you recall that Our Lady said to you on August 22nd 1954, that she was going to come on December 8th in the form of a blue butterfly with two heavenly angels, when we would be on our way to the grotto to put her in place in the 'Promised Land?'

While we were putting the statue in place we felt and heard a beautiful choir of angels. Present that day were: Carlos Castro and friend, Norie and Elizabeth Behrens, Nasira Mistaje, Linda Cabrera, Anita Bustamente, Jose Ramon, my husband Geo, my children and several others. The voices of the heavenly choir impressed us because it was as if the music was coming from the rocks. It was unique and unforgettable!

I must clarify that just before Our Lady's appearance in 1976 we had sensed the beautiful choir of angels and it was the same choir that I had heard on August 22nd, 1954 when I was in my house in San José praying the rosary with a group of young girls. At that time there was a phenomenon made manifest to me. Something like a star fell from the roof and landed on my chest; it was like a dart that passed through my heart and I fell senseless to the floor, as if I was dead. At that moment I was in ecstasy and I had no idea what was happening.

It was certain now that she had appeared to all saying that in the future we would obtain a piece of property. Time had to elapse and during this time I would marry and be the mother of many children. When these children were finally grown up she would appear in the "Promised Land." It was at this time that she said, "When you are on your way to the grotto with my image I shall appear as a blue butterfly." At that time and place incredible things would take place for the eyes of man to behold; all those with me were going to be apostles of her Maternal Heart. They would have to live an apostolic life that would require much sacrifice and humility.

Human nature is weak and some of my followers would betray her and she felt great sorrow in her heart because of this infidelity. She indicated to me that I would have to suffer much and, indeed, I have suffered much on account of these people, but she has given me the strength, courage, and will power to withstand these tests.

As the days passed I received word from the most

Holy Virgin to make arrangements and preparation to take care of the spiritual needs of the people in the area of Betania on February 11th, 1977. She was asking that the sacraments of Baptism, Confirmation, First Communion and Matrimony be administered to them. Our Lady also told me that she would speak to Bishop Bernal about it. I was very preoccupied with this message because it would have to be spontaneous or inspired by Bishop Bernal.

I struggled interiorly with this message for a few days and didn't mention it to anyone. Then Mary appeared to me on January 10th, 1978 and said to me, "My little daughter, I know that you are suffering and that you feel powerless to carry out my request. Let me tell you again that I shall manifest myself to him. Visit the area and try to touch the hearts of the people before the specified date." To follow Our Lady's wishes most of my family with Jesus Andreu went almost daily to Betania.

Then every day for two weeks my husband Geo and Heidi Brillembourg annotated with great anticipation in order to do a good job as their contribution. By the end of January most of the people had been won over to Mary's plan. We entrusted the children to the priest in the Parish of Cua and they cooperated with us.

Four days before the 11th of February Bishop Bernal called me and said, "Maria Esperanza, Our Lady of Lourdes wants me to go to Betania with you and to help you to do what she requested you to do. Why didn't you speak to me about this matter? How did I find out? As you can see Our Lady has her way."

He told me about something that happened to him when he went to Lourdes on a Pilgrimage. Bishop Bernal was leading the procession of the Blessed Sacrament for the sick when a man who was a paralytic got up and began to walk when the Bishop passed by him with the Blessed Sacrament. The man said to him, "The Bishop of the miracle." The Bishop replied, "It is a miracle that I am a bishop." The Bishop laughed and then said to me, "Maria Esperanza, as the years pass by, more and more you will come to realize your mission in life." He went on speaking about the celebrations on the 11th of February and what a beautiful event it was for all my friends and dear companions.

I must add something that impressed me deeply on February 11th and that was the Baptism of the children in the grotto. Accompanying Bishop Bernal was a young boy. I could see he was fervent and close to God. He is now the parish priest of the town of Paracoto.

The priest from Cua could not be in Betania on that day because of a meeting, but there were several other priests present.

There are things that come to my mind at this moment and they are: The Holy Spirit is at work and is communicating His graces and charisms to us because the Virgin Mary is interceding for us. That is why we must praise, praise, praise the Holy Name of God.

Everything that I have lived in Betania seems like a dream to me—the things that have happened and the many people who have been saved. I believe that in the days, months and years to come, this place will be the living example of Christ on earth with His most Holy Mother.

Around the 25th of March, 1978, on Holy Saturday, we met at the grotto to pray and soon we noticed a radiant mist coming towards us from inside the woods and it eventually settled on the top of a tree. The same phenomenon had happened in 1976. I was able to gaze upon the image of my Most Holy Mother with her hands on her chest. Then her hands opened up and I saw what appeared to be rays coming from her hands. They came directly towards us bathing us with light in such a fashion that Nasira Mistaje uttered a cry saying, "Everything is burning up!" Actually, the whole area appeared to be on fire. It was beautiful! The sun began to gyrate and everyone was shouting with emotion. I couldn't say anything and spontaneously I fell to the ground. I felt everything around me moving as I was raised into the air. Then I heard the soft, tender voice of Our Lady within me saying, "Little daughter, this is not a dream; my presence among you is real. Obey and follow faithfully this Mother so that you may be happy for all eternity. Accept the arduous task of bringing my message of love and reconciliation to the people of all nations. You will suffer, but what joy and happiness it will be to see that you have been faithful to your Mother. I take you by the hand."

I felt that I was gently touching the ground again. It was then that I realized that my daughter Maria Garcia was weeping inconsolably because she saw me in mid-air and didn't know what to do to get me down again. My Godchild Jacqueline Leon was also very frightened. The event startled all present.

I was told to take a piece of paper by the people present and all of those present signed it and it was later given to Bishop Pio Bello Ricardo.

I want to make it clear that the type of fire we witnessed that day in the woods was also repeated from the seventh to the last apparition on March 25th, 1984.

Finally, I wish to affirm that my Mother has promised me that both she and Jesus will appear in Betania in the same year—1987. It is very compromising to speak of this, but I have to be faithful to my Mother's word and to the word of her Divine Son Jesus. I feel it is the truth and I have offered my life, as a victim soul, for priests and religious throughout the world. It is for them that I offer all that is in my heart because I so love the Catholic Church, the Mother Church, the Holy Church. It is the Church that I have loved since my childhood and I have always respected those priests and religious who have consecrated their lives in God's service for their fellow man. It makes me tremble deeply when I realize how bravely they have taken up the cross when they heard and answered God's call.

Thanks be to the Lord for all His benefits to my soul! Blessed may you be, my greatest love! I wish to remain before the Blessed Sacrament in the ciborium day and night, and to live only for you.

Bless me!
In Obedience,
Maria Esperanza de Bianchini

OFFICIAL STATEMENT OF GEO BIANCHINI GIANI

Maria Esperanza's husband, Geo Bianchini Giani was also asked to share with Bishop Pio Bello Ricardo what he remembered about the early days of the apparitions at Betania and this is a summary of his statement to the bishop.

I feel the immense urge to leave a written testimony of a most wonderful event. It will fill many human beings with immense satisfactions, and even more to future generations because they will fully understand the importance and meaning.

My name is Geo Bianchini Giani. I am an Italian who was born and raised in Italy and the husband of Maria Esperanza Medrano de Bianchini. We have seven children, six daughters and one son. We live in Caracas and soon Maria and I will have been married twenty-eight years. My work is in the field of construction.

For many years it was our dream to purchase the land for Betania and it brought great happiness when in March of 1974 with two other couples we bought it. We learned later that this parcel of land had a grotto and a spring. What a surprise! It corresponded perfectly with the information given to my wife when she was a young girl.

Soon we got into the habit of visiting Betania regularly to work in fixing it up, taking care of the animals, or just for the happiness we found in being there.

Most of 1975 and 1976 we spent in Rome, Italy taking care of my mother who was old and infirm.

In 1977 when we returned to Caracas we were soon in the habit of visiting and staying at Betania.

On March 25th, 1977 there were about thirty people in front of the grotto praying the rosary when suddenly my wife and some of the others indicated that they were seeing the Blessed Mother, and by the way they described the incident it was impossible for me to doubt them. Even though I wasn't present I wasn't disappointed because my faith is such that I have always believed without seeing. I had never prayed to see or have supernatural experiences. I trust God knows what is best for me.

With the passing of time, I have seen many exterior manifestations of the kindness and love of the Holy Virgin such as: the vision of the blue butterfly, the aroma of roses and lilies, spikenard and incense, colors and lights, cool breezes, and all without any explanation. I want to make it clear that I am not a visionary nor do I have any special powers. I am, and I insist on being very realistic, and at times this makes it difficult for me to get in touch with the Divine.

It was like a dream to me as we were making preparations to commemorate the eighth anniversary of Our Lady appearing under the title of "Mary, Virgin and Mother of Reconciliation of All People." This place would be a place of prayer and a refuge for all people coming here to find consolation and love and to be able to live in complete harmony and not allow any differences to separate them.

The Mass on March 25th, 1984 was celebrated by Monsignor Laborem, and the first time the youth choir participated in the singing of the Mass. It was a real treat for the one hundred and fifty people present, in fact, it was like a retreat for them with most participating in the reception of the Eucharist.

After the celebration of the Mass there followed a period of relaxation and most of the people were having a picnic and chatting with each other.

Approximately, at 3:00 p.m. the same afternoon, we heard the voice of a child excitedly saying, "The Blessed Mother is present among the foliage at the top of the spring's grotto." We all ran immediately to the grotto and there we could gaze upon her figure about one hundred and fifty meters away from us. She seemed to be like a marble statue and I recognized her as "Our Lady of Lourdes." All who were with me felt it was Our Lady of Lourdes too. Our Lady did not move and stayed among us for fifteen minutes.

What a moving experience! We all felt so happy! Spontaneously all present began praying, weeping, beseeching and praising God. Some began inquiring to see if there was something to produce such an effect and I was sad when Our Lady disappeared because I was distracted and did not see how or when she disappeared.

Until 6:15 p.m. Our Lady appeared seven times at the grotto and on one occasion I saw Our Lady appear and for two of the apparitions I saw her disappear.

34

Our Lady's image was clear and perfect amidst the background of the dark green woods. In the foliage was the figure of Our Lady, as if emerging from a dense mist and when she disappeared it seemed as if Our Lady was being absorbed from behind. While the image was present to us one had the impression that she was moving and approaching us and when this happened many shouted with joy.

During the second apparition, I clearly saw a light that was much brighter than her figure on the right side of Mary's chest. In the fifth apparition I could see a little white circle coming out of her left arm that I thought to be the head of a child. I could not distinguish her features, but others said they were able to see them; however, I, only saw the distinct shape of a woman with a white cloak down to her feet. She was of average height. The farther away that I moved the better I could see her.

When the apparitions ended it was getting late and the sun had already set. There was no doubt that Our Lady had permitted about one hundred people present to see her. At the tenth apparition Our Lady appeared for more than one half hour and all contradictory opinions of natural analysis or incredulity disappeared and all were ready to testify fully to this miraculous happening. They were more than willing to confirm what had taken place by writing in the book for that purpose.

I am going to describe something else. About two weeks before March 25th, 1984, Our Lady appeared in the same place and under similar circumstances to two women about sixty years old. One of the women takes care of the property at Betania. On Friday morning around 9:00 a.m. on March 9th, they went to the grotto area to get some water. They recognized Our Lady immediately. Apprehensively, they told me the next day about the apparition because they felt I wouldn't believe them and would laugh at them. I went with them to the grotto because that is where she appears, but we saw nothing. The caretaker was upset but I calmed her down and told her that I truly believed that she had seen Our Lady, and that she wasn't telling a lie. During the next week she told me that she had seen her several times and that her sister, our tractor operator, and five people in all had seen Mary during the week.

With all these events, I consider these apparitions to be of great importance. It is not and it cannot be taken as an isolated event.

All of us present for an apparition received the privilege of seeing Our Lady, but also the responsibility of changing our lives and in the days to follow to become messengers and witnesses to all people and to share the blessings and graces that Our Lady bestows on those present during an apparition.

I am well acquainted with Our Lady's apparitions throughout the world and I believe that appearing to over one hundred people the Most Holy Virgin is accomplishing her work of love among her children without distinction of race, color, or religion so that all may be reconciled and love one another. The commandment of God says, "Love one another as I have loved you."

This is my testimony and I hope it may be helpful to all those souls who wish to find in it a motive of intimate satisfaction and at the same time it should help us to overcome the coldness of our hearts.

Geo Bianchini Giani

Chapter 5

What Is Our Lady's Message?

5

What Is Our Lady's Message in Betania?

One of the characteristics of the spirituality of Senora Bianchini is the reception of the "messages." There are many—let us look at some of them:

The First Message

"Little daughter, I am giving you a glimpse of heaven....Lourdes....Betania of Venezuela....there is a place for all, not only Catholics...it is for everyone. There is no distinction of classes, nationalities, religions. This land is for the gathering of all those that wish to enter there!

"It is your Mother who gives herself, as in Lourdes, Fatima, Pilar of Zaragoza, Guanare,....as in many other places where I continue to give myself. But remember: Here will be the light of the east.

"This place will be a place of belief, of prayer, of faith, love, and charity. It will be for the ennoblement of the hearts of whoever draws near...a renewal of the city of God. I wish to create here, in this place, a replica of my holy fountain. Lourdes does not need more said for it, there I live, that is the truth. Thus

I will live in Venezuela, in the Betania of a more powerful day. The maternal water that I bring is the water of life; it is the water of health, of baptism. It is the origin of your life in Christ; it will be the water for pardon, that will wash away your faults and will renew you. Even more will you praise my name with the Hail Mary which is a simple salutation. Our encounter will be more alive, more moving, and again you will be able to rekindle again the faith in the hearts of your brothers and sisters.

"Little sons and daughters, here you have me among you, so that you experience me and contemplate me among bushes and trees of this little wood that I have chosen. Here all of you will find health, peace, and love of this Mother, who, with the spring of water, desires to renew you. Because the love of my Heavenly Father, that of my Divine Son and Holy Spirit, the Consoler, burns eternally in your hearts. They inflame you with the holy fire that the supernatural life communicates to you, the life of grace, the Divine Life. May there be participation in the Divine Love, in the Divinity. Do you understand me well? Do you know what it is that I want to point out to you?

"It is for this, that, as Mother, as the Immaculate Mother, Mediatrix of all graces, that I call you to this place...so that my union with you may be more intimate and vital, through the Holy Spirit, permitting you to live deeply the spirit of the Gospel. Yes, children, I am your Mother, furthermore, I am the refuge of sinners and the help of all Christians.

"It is for this that I invite you to come frequently

to tell me what you feel, your preoccupations, your troubles, your complaints, in short, all the hopes you have, the doubts or anxieties. I invite you especially to consecrate your hearts to me, so that I may renew them.

"Give yourselves over unconditionally into my maternal arms, live as in infancy, as little children, so that I may hold you in my protection. With my Immaculate glance hidden within you as in the little home of Nazareth, you can begin your apostolic preparation, being able, little by little, to overcome so many things, being able to receive each day the Eucharist, as the food of souls and so be strengthened by my Divine Son."

The Second Message

"Little children, here in this place you will be able to break the ties that confound you today and prevent you from appreciating the call that we give you. My Divine Son and I, His Mother, give ourselves to your hearts in order that you might do with a generous and right spirit what the Father asks, that is, to save all His children from the mockery and derision of the hypocrites of these apocalyptic times.

"He, in His infinite mercy, will strengthen the steps of those who will rise up in a service of continual self-giving, of dialoging, of teaching an appreciation of human values of a people. My people seek the truth of a just and fair teaching with moral values that will consolidate people and nations in one simple fraternal embrace.

"I come to direct all who wish to take refuge in my maternal heart; it is for that, that I have taken possession of you. I hope to lead you and that you will call my children to this place of the holy waters of my hopes and that it will become a place of harmony, refreshment, and peace for those who come in search of this Mother, the shepherdess of souls. I have come, too, to lighten the burdens of my priestly sons because it is they, the ones who responding to my call, will have to make of my place, chosen for these times of great calamities for humanity, the sacred enclosure where all my children will find refuge, to rebuild the walls of the triumphant New Jerusalem where all have to be saved by the faith, love, and truth of a people crying out for justice.

"Now, meditate in silence and submit to prayer that you may comprehend and accept my presence among you. I say this especially to religious, my consecrated priests and missionary sisters—that they may enter wholeheartedly into prayer and contemplation which is so necessary in this hour so decisive for humanity.

"Action and work are the axis but without prayer works are ruined. It is important, even necessary, to consider the vows. Pastors take your flocks and form of them one big human family. Behold here pastors who are blessed with good possibilities in their flocks, it is a beautiful apostolate and it needs prayer to keep them united to my Son.

"It is for this that I beg you, my children, do not stop adoring; you cannot stray from my Maternal heart. You are consecrated religious and receive orders

44

from your superiors—you must remain faithful, perservering in your apostolic work for the benefit of God's people.

"I, my children, will remain faithful until the end, following in the footsteps of my Divine Son. You have a great responsibility. You know that willpower and good intention is the basis. Jesus is there with sacrifice and He reveals Himself in the silence of the temple of each heart of His ministers. In adoration He becomes present; it is the proper surrender to Christ, My Divine Son. But in the strength of the outpouring of the Holy Spirit it will become true in you in an exceptional way—you will be one alone with Him. Lo! The beauty and grandeur of what it means to be a priest."

The Third Message

"Children: you will not be able to be perfect because, as long as there are flesh and blood, you all have to pass through stages, years that will be instruction. With that you will be acquiring the model of Christian perfection, Christ, my Divine Son, in all of you.

"You must have a hunger for God and a hunger for His gifts, and for this Mother that continues to give herself each day, in every part of the world so that people may be saved. In this land, this 'promised land,' hunger for its children to be renewed so that they may be able, together with their brothers and sisters who will come from afar, to find refuge here.

"Children, as Mary, Mother Reconciler of People,

I come to reconcile them, to seek them out, to give them faith, which has disappeared in the noise and din of an atomic awakening which is at the point of bursting out. Passions, power, material wealth have turned them cold, lukewarm and egotistical, behold the complaint of a great evil that is covering the earth with shadows. The inferno raised among men must be extinguished through the medium of kindness, love and truth of the heart of this Mother. There must be pardon, reflecting that only love can save everyone. There is a great need for social justice, a redeeming spirituality, healthy and understood. Only in this way will destruction among brothers and sisters be avoided.

"Who works with determination and dedication in the service of the Lord, teaching His doctrine and His Gospel—this one has succeeded in growing in virtue and sanctity. He merits in a special way the graces and blessings of the Father.

"Behold the great triumph of a way that unifies, reestablishes, weighs the merit of the multitudes that will be arriving at my place chosen for these times. Conversion of the sinner, health of body and soul, priestly and religious vocations, holy marriages, families renewed in the faith, charisms of the Holy Spirit working in all who draw near in humility— these will happen! Those who are repentant and who weep over their errors may turn their eyes to the grotto of my apparition, asking me for pardon; they will receive an abundance of grace, their souls will remain pure and clean like the day they were cleansed in holy Baptism. All will rise with my Son!

"Little children, I call you this day to the fullness of life, that you may live with a conscience clear and responsible for your entrusted mission, with the theological virtues of faith, hope, and charity. I especially recommend to you purity of intention, humility, simplicity and obedience to the responsibility contracted with the Lord. Promise to stay on the right road of innocence.

"How lovely is the beauty of innocent children, of those who live spontaneously, naturally without harming or injuring any human being, on the contrary, helping, inviting all to be brothers and sisters, to live life by example, in the love of the Lord, our Father, that He may give us being, His life."

The Fourth Message

"Little children, today, healthful for your souls you must contribute to helping me build my house in this place. A refuge of a Mother with the title, 'Mary, Reconciler of People and Nations.' Pray, meditate, and nourish yourselves with the bread of the Eucharist which gives you supernatural life. Be what you are: strong souls, healthy and strong, to combat with the weapons of love since it is love by which you are going to penetrate hearts and the consciences of all my children, dwellers of these lands, in a summons, an outcry shouting: 'Rise up, the hour has come for rebuilding the moral values of a People of God.'

"I want to be known, I repeat to you, under the name of Virgin and Mother, Reconciler for the People because man needs to find himself. He needs to see in each human being his or her own brother or sister. Ideologies may be respected because it is respect that is due to one's self, to each one, to recognize each one as a member of one same family, the family of God.

"Little children, all rise to a single ideal, struggle for the poorest and the most abandoned, struggle for the new generation that must grow and develop in a healthy environment.

"Yes, my children, learn the value of each person in his or her own milieu where he or she lives and moves, with his or her way of thinking as well as in the negative side of their surroundings. Learn to value these people in order to help them to fight against the evil that surrounds them, drawing them forward to live in a healthy atmosphere in spiritual peace as God, the Father, wishes to save you all by faith. It is man's answer in the midst of the structure of society, being sure that God has created you.

"Little children, I am your Mother, and I come to seek you so that you may prepare yourselves to be able to bring my message of reconciliation. There is coming the great moment of a great day of light. The consciences of this beloved people must be violently shaken so that they may 'put their house in order' and offer to Jesus the just reparation for the daily infidelities that are committed on the part of sinners.

"Little children, I want to take possession of your hearts! To give you in the Holy Spirit the gift of understanding that you may find the profound

48

significance of my presence among you. I am offering you the opportunity of the great promise that one day my Divine Son will make known to you. It is essentially important in these times: 'The Reconciliation of the Universe.' Oh may it be...people with God, and people with each other!

"Lo, this Mother who is pleading as the poorest of women, the littlest, the most humble, but the most pure; she wishes to transmit to you again the purity of heart, simplicity, loyalty, obedience to the service of your brothers and sisters, prudence, and still more, constant zeal for the works of our Mother, the Church. Today there is need of giving testimony with your life and your faith in God so that this Mother may be able to prepare you for the apostolate. Prepare you, yes, and the invitation is commendable and assuredly valid if you desire it. With a recommendation for perseverance, proceed and put it into practice."

The Fifth Message

"Little children, if one calls, knocks, insists and perseveres, the door of my holy mountain will be opened and you will be able to live taking water from my living fountain. What this Mother means is just that. May you keep at heart my message, meditating on it. May you put my requests into practice.

"Children, I wait for you. I continue waiting for all of you. May there remain no one whatsoever in the land that does not come to visit me. I am the Mother of God. I have called you to this little piece of land.

I am the same Mother, under different titles but I am Mary, of Nazareth, the Mother of Suffering. No one was as brave as I was, nor gave more proof of love to God, our Father. Little children, I am the Mother of Good Counsel, Mediator, who is trying to persuade you to listen to the call. My message is of faith, love and hope. More than anything, it brings reconciliation between people and nations. It is the only thing that can save this century from war and eternal death. My children, there rests in your hands the salvation of a people that pleads for justice.

"Good little children, take possession of the place in realizing the work of the great Temple.

"You young people, I invite you to work with vigor and good purpose to teach the ones who do not know. Remain firm and stalwart as soldiers taking care of what pertains to you by law.

"And to all: fathers, mothers, unite in one single embrace so that your children may reap the harvest of the sowing of good dispositions—the service of God! Little children; today, in these times, He with Me, wishes to renew consciences because man is abusing the graces received and is heading toward perdition. If a change does not come and a conversion of life, one will perish under the fire, war and death. We want to hold off the evil that is oppressing you in being rebellious and to conquer the darkness of the oppression of the enemy.

"It is for that reason that again, in this century, my Divine Son rises up so that you may follow in His wake as a shepherd of souls. It is to obtain the alliance of peace among brothers and sisters and to

50

keep your hearts as clean temples; to guard in silence the inspiration of the Voice of Wisdom, learning with them that silence is spiritual gold which comes to each being with healthy joy. May His Word as Teacher be listened to. Await the call with due devotion."

Chapter 6

My First Trip
To
Betania

6

My First Trip To Betania

I can remember very clearly my interview with Mother M. Euphrasia, the head of the Sisters of St. Joseph of Boston, on the day when I went for my initial interview to enter that Order. One of her questions to me was, "Teresa, are you sure you want to be a diocesan Sister of St. Joseph and not a missionary sister of some kind?" She then went on to inform me that if I became a "diocesan" sister *I would never be able to leave the Boston area.* Little did the Reverend Mother Euphrasia realize that I wasn't really certain I wanted to be any kind of a sister at that particular moment.

September 8th, 1953 I entered the Sisters of Saint Joseph and on March 19th, 1954 I received the habit of the Sisters of Saint Joseph and sat nervously in the Chapel waiting to receive my new name. What would it be? Richard Cardinal Cushing, finally, came to me and said, "Teresa Catherine Sims you will now be known in religion as Sister Margaret Catherine Sims." Whew! What a relief! It was a name I could pronounce, in fact, it was the name I had prayed I would receive.

On August 15th, 1959 I made my Final Vows as a Sister of Saint Joseph and three days later went to my new mission in Santa Fe, New Mexico. After spending thirteen very happy and fruitful years teaching in New Mexico, I returned to the Boston area in August 1972.

While in New Mexico I had become involved in the Charismatic Renewal at the Monastery of Our Lady of Guadalupe in Pecos, New Mexico, and shortly after returning to Boston I found myself traveling throughout the New England area giving talks and seminars on Life in the Holy Spirit.

In the Fall of 1975 I began a new apostolate, full time, giving retreats and spiritual direction to people in the Charismatic Renewal. Now, instead of traveling throughout New England, I was traveling throughout the United States.

In May 1983 I attended a Leadership Conference for the Charismatic Renewal at the College of Steubenville in Ohio, and at the opening talk Father Michael Scanlon shared with us his experiences in Medugorje. It was the first time I heard the word, but even then my spirit reacted to it with excitement. I couldn't read enough about it and in those days all we had were a few newspaper articles written by Theresa Kaminsky. My first visit to Medugorje was in May, 1984 and since that first trip I have made forty two pilgrimages there and given retreats to thousands of pilgrims.

So many times in the past thirty five years I have thought about my first interview with Mother Euphrasia and her telling me that if I entered the

Sisters of Saint Joseph of Boston I would never leave the Boston area. What a sense of humor the Lord has because I have spent more time outside the Boston diocese than I have in it.

On January 3rd, 1990 I found myself on the way to Caracas, Venezuela with Sister Frances Scribner, smsm, to check on what was taking place at "Betania." I had left from "Bethany Hill" in Framingham, Massachusetts to go to "Bethany" the "Promised Land" of Maria Esperanza de Bianchini in Venzuela. What did the Lord and His Blessed Mother have in store for me there?

On the 5th of January we traveled about two hours by "taxi" from our hotel in Caracas to Betania. After investigating the grotto and the "spring", Sister Frances and I washed our faces with water coming down from between the rocks. We didn't realize that we were supposed to have been drinking it.

There were two houses on the premises and I just presumed we would find Maria, the visionary, in one of them. After much confusion I found out that Maria actually lives in Caracas and only comes to Betania on Holy Days and weekends. The caretaker of the property was very nice to us and when he found out we were sisters from Boston he gave us the Bishop's telephone number and said to call him when we arrived back at the hotel in Caracas.

The Holy Spirit was really going ahead and preparing the way for us. Bishop Pio Bello Ricardo was busy packing for his vacation and too busy to see us. However, he said, "Sister Margaret, this is Maria Esperanza's telephone number. Call and tell her I told you to call her."

I called Maria's home and her son-in-law, Juan Carlos, answered the phone. When I told him that the Bishop had told me to call and arrange an appointment with her, he consulted Maria Esperanza and she said to tell us she would send a car to bring us to her home the next day. It was Sunday, January 6th, the Feast of the Epiphany.

Her husband Geo was the first to greet us and gradually we met many members of her family. They told us that Maria Esperanza had not gone to Betania the day before because she wasn't feeling well, but she would be down to speak to us in a few moments.

Maria finally came down the circular staircase and she reached out to embrace us. She thanked us for coming to see her, and especially for having visited Betania. Maria beams when she talks about Our Lady and what has taken place at Betania.

As we sat informally around her living room, Maria Esperanza began to share Our Lady's messages of Betania with us. In Betania, Our Lady comes as "Mary, Virgin and Mother of Reconciliation." Maria stressed the importance of *forgiveness* if there is to be true love, because without forgiveness and love there will never be true reconciliation.

Maria explained, "Our Lady loves us just as we are with our weaknesses and strengths. She has come to be with us to increase and strengthen our faith, and she is calling us to serve others with simplicity and humility, as you and I are reaching out and serving each other today. Love is so important. Our

Mother says, 'Where there is love there is the salvation of mankind. Love! It is so important! Peace! I love peace! Love! I love love! I love all of God's people.'

"I'm happy that you are here and I can spend this time with you, because I believe that it is not just you that I am speaking to, but all the people you represent. Some of the people you will reach will be very strong while others will be very weak and it is important that we touch all people with Our Lady's message. She wants to reconcile *all* people.

"When I am speaking to people I like to take my time and to try to understand the personalities of the other people. In this way we come to understand others and not to make judgements about them."

At this point in our conversation Maria asked me to put the video camera down, and when I did she said to Sister Frances, "Sister, what happened to you when you were twenty five years old?" After a few moments sister explained that she had spent part of the year in the hospital and in a body cast. Maria smiled, and then went on to describe a man, and asked Sister Frances if she knew the man whom she was describing. Sister replied, "Yes, the man you described is my father." Maria Esperanza then shared with Sister Frances, that at the time of her hospitalization, her father, who was in heaven, interceded for her and because of his love and intercession on her behalf, she was alive and able to walk today. Needless to say, sister was deeply touched by this revelation.

The sharing continued and after a few minutes, Maria asked me to put the camera down again. This time Maria began to describe a woman, and then said, "Sister Margaret, do you know this woman?" I told Maria that the woman she had described was the only mother I had known. My mother died when I was an infant and I was brought up by her sister, "Mom Sims." Again Maria smiled and said, "Sister Margaret, you travel quite frequently, and when you pick up your suitcase to board an airplane, your mother is there with you, watching over you, protecting you and interceding in heaven for you."

Before leaving the home of Maria Esperanza, Sister Frances and I knelt down in front of Maria and asked Maria to pray with us and for us. In the middle of the prayer, Maria stopped for a moment and it was truly a moment of great grace, because as we knelt at her feet, Maria had an apparition. Our Lady appeared to Maria with a message for us:

"My daughters, my love for you is a Mother's love. Your vocation is such an important one. In today's world it is necessary to have priests and sisters, who have consecrated and dedicated their lives to serving my Son, Jesus.

"So many people in the world are confused today because they do not have anyone to reach out to them and to teach them religious truths. Be generous in serving the Lord and reaching out to God's people. God wants you to touch the hearts of all your brothers and sisters, but especially the sisters in your communities. Love the apostolic work you do for Jesus. Walk among the people of God, rich or poor, serving them as my Son and His apostles did while they were on earth. Walk in my Son's footsteps.

"I am your Mother and I want you to breathe in the freshness of Betania's air and to take into the depths of your heart the happiness and peace that you found in Betania."

Maria then embraced Sister Frances and me and was very happy that Our Lady had given her a message for us.

Chapter 7

A Pilgrimage To Betania

7

A Pilgrimage To Betania

When we were leaving Maria Esperanza's home she said, "Sister Margaret, I shall see you again, because Our Lady desires that you bring many pilgrims to Betania."

In my heart I always knew that I would return to Betania but I just didn't know WHEN. My plan and will was to wait until a church was erected in the "promised land." How easy it is to take pilgrims to a holy place when there is a church, priests, and sisters to help you! How often God's schedule and ours is different!

Just before Christmas of 1991 I began to sense that Our Lady was beginning to nudge me to start making preparations to return to Betania, and this time to take others with me.

When? Since the sixteenth anniversary of the apparitions in Betania would be on March 25th, that seemed like an appropriate time. In prayer, I began to receive messages from Our Lady such as: "Take the material that you have on Betania and delve into it. It will be an enlightening experience for you. Listen, as I speak to you and reveal my plan for the retreat to you."

"Spend time in prayer to prepare for taking my 'loved ones' to Betania. My Son's mercy and forgiveness and my Mother's love will permeate the group. Maria Esperanza will speak words of wisdom to many in the group. Listen so that you will be able to live the messages that she will give to you."

(Personal Journal - March 9th, 1992)

"In Betania you will begin that walk in deeper love and understanding of the Father's unconditional love. Love Me! Love my sons and daughters. Be strong in this love. The love I give to you, share with all people. Do not opt or choose whom to love, but rather love all."

(Personal Journal - March 11, 1992)

"My Spirit, the Holy Spirit, will be a real presence during the retreat in Betania. Let the Spirit move and flow and there will be an abundance of mercy and love flowing in and through all those on the retreat. If you remain open and allow the Holy Spirit and my Mother to lead you, great and powerful things will happen on this Pilgrimage."

(Personal Journal - March 15th, 1992)

Needless to say, as the time approached I was really looking forward to the pilgrimage and my return to Betania. Thirty-five of us left from all parts of the United States and I must admit that I really had my doubts when Carol Cohoon, our Travel Director at Medugorje Messengers, said to me, "The airplanes from Miami, New York, California and Boston will all arrive between 3:30 p.m. and 4:00 p.m." Who was she kidding? Having traveled extensively, forty-two times to Medugorje, I know it is a miracle when one plane arrives on time, never mind four planes arriving on time. Miracle of miracles they all were on time, in fact, some were even early.

After going through Customs and "collecting" all my pilgrims" I started to look for our guide. A smiling young man came up to me and said, "Sister Margaret, I will be your guide for the week and my name is 'Jesus.'" How could we go wrong with 'Jesus" as our guide!

First day in Betania:

Since it was a two hour ride from our hotel in Caracas to Betania, we left at 9:30 a.m. packed and prepared to spend the day there. When we arrived approximately two hundred people had gathered around the grotto area and were praying and sharing with each other. Our pilgrims did the same until it was time for Father Vincent Von Euw, our priest on the pilgrimage, to celebrate Mass for us—our first Mass in Betania.

After Mass, we learned that there was going to be a midnight Mass and it would be at that Mass that Maria Esperanza would probably have her apparition. What should we do? It was only 1:00 p.m. After conferring with 'Jesus," our guide, arrangements were made to return to our hotel in Caracas for a few hours rest, something to eat, and a change of clothes. What a surprise! When we returned to Betania around 9:00 p.m., there were about fifteen thousand people there and most of them had little children with them. Every place you looked there were blankets spread out, people on cots and lawn chairs, praying and singing. One had to be careful walking not to step on a sleeping child.

People processed around the altar and grotto all night praying the rosary and the Stations of the Cross. During the night the local people prayed and sang and many witnessed to physical healings that had taken place after they drank some water from the spring at the grotto.

Some of our pilgrims had taken blankets and pillows from the hotel thinking they might take a nap after the midnight Vigil Mass and before the first Mass the next day on the feast of the Annunciation. How wrong they were! It was difficult to find a place to stand, never mind spreading out a blanket.

Second Day in Betania -
The Feast of the Annunciation:

There were several Masses celebrated on the Feast of the Annunciation beginning at 7:00 a.m., including one in English at 10:30 a.m. celebrated by Fr. Vincent. The main Mass at noon was attended by Maria Esperanza, the visionary. After the Mass at noon, Maria spoke to the congregation and described Our Blessed Mother's apparition and her message of reconciliation.

Maria Esperanza's Message to all
on March 25th, 1992

"Good afternoon to all my brothers and sisters. Our Heavenly Mother has been appearing here in Betania for over sixteen years now, having visited us for the first time on March 25th, 1976. She appeared at the grotto in a brilliant light and with rays of light coming from her hands to shine on all of us with peace. It is the peace and light that we need to strengthen our faith and to heal us. Our Mother is there to help us in all our needs.

"So many people attended that beautiful Mass last night looking for our beautiful Mother to open up her heart to them. Your Mother is a loving, caring, generous mother. How beautiful and sweet is the Immaculate Heart of our Mother, Mary! Oh Mary, if all your sons and daughters could see you as I see you! It would only take one glance at your beauty and the whole world would be renewed and saved. Oh, if only all your sons and daughters could see and feel your holy presence.

"My brothers and sisters, I am so excited that Our Lady, my Mother, has been coming here to Betania for over sixteen years! How happy I always am when I can come to Betania! I am so happy to see so many of you here today and to know that you come from all parts of the world.

"I am willing to suffer all kinds of tribulations so that people will be able to hear the message of the

Gospel, and to receive the blessings of God that our Mother, Mary, brings to us.

"God is with us and present to the world in His successor Pope John Paul II, who travels throughout the entire world reaching out and touching all people, rich or poor, as he walks in the footsteps of Jesus Christ and His apostles. What an example Pope John Paul II is for each one of us! We should pray daily for him so that he will have strong health so that he can carry out God's plan.

"We have laid the 'cornerstone' in what will eventually be the church of Mary, Virgin and Mother of Reconciliation of All People. Some day you will be able to pray to her Son Jesus in this church.

"St. Peter was the first Pope of our Church—the Catholic Church—the Apostolic Church—the Universal Church—the Roman Catholic Church. How beautiful is our Church! The Church is all people. It doesn't matter where you come from or what race you belong to, the most important thing is that we can embrace each other and receive the Body and Blood of our Savior, Jesus Christ. How beautiful it is to rest at His Mother's feet!

"Mary is appearing more often in these times to teach us and to show us how to live and how to keep the commandments of her Divine Son.

"Jesus Christ uttered from the cross, 'I Thirst!' It is not water that Jesus thirsts for today, but He thirsts for souls. He wants you! He wants your soul! I pray that each one of you may never turn your back on the Eucharist and I pray daily for you to come ever closer to the Eucharistic Body and Blood of Jesus

Christ. The Eucharist is the food necessary for you if you are to follow in the footsteps of Jesus. The Eucharist is the fundamental basis for all Catholics. It is the most important thing in the lives of all God's children.

"The Eucharist can change and transform our lives so that we are able to give up our sinful ways. It makes us strong and lights up the pathway to heaven for us. Eucharist and charity go hand in hand. Without charity it is very difficult to enter the Kingdom of heaven.

"Jesus is waiting for us in all the churches throughout the world. He is waiting with open arms for us to come to Him with our problems, fears and sicknesses, and He promises us that we shall rise above them just as He did. He holds out His hand to us so that we too may rise from the darkness. He is Risen!

"I know that this is true because in Betania many times My Mother has shared this with me.

"For a long time Mary, Virgin and Mother of Reconciliation of All People came, and only I could see her, but now many people have seen her. How many children—Infirm—sick—unbelievers—have seen our Mother and now they are healed and now they believe.

"There is a spiritual revolution going on in the world today. Our Holy Mother wants to touch every son and daughter. She comes with Jesus in her arms and she wants to give Him to us. At Bethlehem she gave her Son to the world and today she wants to give Him to each one of us, her children.

"Mary, our Mother wants us to pray at all times, to

pray unceasingly, because she knows that prayer will make us strong and it will take away our fears, and anxieties.

"Pray for priests and religious because they have dedicated their lives, and although they have given much they have received many spiritual gifts from God. We have to pray so that these spiritual gifts will be strengthened and used generously. If we do this the Gospel and Voice of Jesus will be heard throughout the world.

"Mary, our Mother is the reconciler of all people and she comes so that we may be reconciled with her Son and with all people. If we are to have peace it is necessary to be reconciled with brothers and sisters. Open your arms and hearts and receive the sweetness and love of the Immaculate Heart and the Sacred Heart as their love reaches out to you.

"Our Blessed Mother is reconciling the whole world—brothers—sisters—families—nations. We must be obedient to her plan. Reconcile! Our Lady has said, 'If you say that you can't be reconciled, it is not that you can't be reconciled, but rather that you won't be reconciled.'

"To the priests Our Mother says: 'Be obedient to my Son's plan for you and I will be there with you.' God chooses the plan and the way for each one of us.

"Mary is present with us at all times. Her presence is there when we eat, go to school, pray. She is present with us in times of joy and sadness, peace and unrest, health and sickness. Our Mother wants her children to know she is there with each one of you.

"Thank you, Father, for all your gifts and blessings!

"Thank you, Mary, for coming to Betania for so many years!

"I am crying right now, at this moment, because I feel the presence of my Mother within my heart. How beautiful it is! How beautiful it is to live one's life with Our Lady! This life is a life of peace and reconciliation.

"Jesus Christ, when He walked the road of Calvary to the Cross, walked it with His Mother, Mary. She was with Him and she will be with you too. On the Cross Jesus said to His Mother, 'Here is your son.' and to St. John, the beloved apostle, 'Here is your Mother.' She is our Mother! Jesus Christ gave His Mother to us and we should be obedient to her will and to follow her guidance. She is our Mother!

"If someone loves you deeply then it is important that they also love your children, therefore, if we love Jesus Christ then we must love His Mother Mary.

"By the power of the Holy Spirit Mary brought Jesus to us in Bethlehem and today by the power of the Holy Spirit she continues to bring Jesus into our lives.

"Thank you, Jesus, for your blessings! Thank you Jesus for your Mother! Thank you, Jesus! Thank you, Mary!"

Third Day in Betania

After the Mass at noon on the feast of the Annunciation I was able to talk to Maria Esperanza and I was happy that she remembered me. I asked her if she would be able to speak to my group because in prayer I felt the Lord and His Blessed Mother had revealed that Maria would have a message for them.

Maria smiled as only she can, nodded and said, "Yes, Sister Margaret, I shall speak to your group either Thursday or Friday before you leave Betania because for several days Our Lady and her Son have been giving me messages for them."

On Thursday when we returned to Betania it truly was a day of *many* graces and blessings. In the morning Father Vincent found a little place in the picnic area and most of the group took advantage of the opportunity to receive the sacrament of Reconciliation. Since there were very few people in the area today it was a time of prayer, reflection and reconciliation.

Maria Esperanza invited us to have Mass on the patio of her home in Betania and after Mass she spoke to the group and it was at this time that she had a message for the group and special messages for some of the pilgrims.

Maria's Message to the Group:

"Blessings on all of you present here today. I welcome all of you who have traveled a great distance to Betania to honor Mary, Virgin and Mother of Reconciliation of All People.

"Here our Blessed Mother has opened her heart and covers us with a beautiful mantle. She wants to fill us with the love of her heart. She wants to free you and draw you into her embracing heart and have you accept her message of love, reconciliation and peace, because without reconciliation peace is impossible.

74

"It is necessary that we live this message of reconciliation and to have peace and justice. The heart of Our Lady at this moment is filled with happiness and contentment and she is rejoicing as she looks at each one of you.

"Our Mother looks on you as her children, her little ones, because the child is the most beautiful one who exists because of its innocence and openness. The innate freshness, which is so spontaneous and natural is what Our Lady wishes to bestow upon you. It is up to you to accept and to respond to her beautiful graces and also to the charisms of the Holy Spirit. The Holy Spirit radiates light and graces on the whole world in order that all of God's children receive the fragrance of Mary's graces, the perfume of beautiful roses, the flowers of joy into our hearts.

"My mother named me Esperanza, 'hope', and it is with hope in the name of Mary, Virgin and Mother of Reconciliation of All People, that I welcome you in Betania.

"Betania is the land of Our Mother. It is Mary's land and also the land of all her children who come to Betania to pray.

"Our Mother is so lovely, so generous, so radiant. She thanks each one of you for coming here to Betania.

"We have just celebrated Mass together and received the Body and Blood of Jesus Christ. He is our food! He is our strength! He is our protection! Jesus is always present, the Son of God, the Teacher of all teachers, the vital spiritual force of all people in the Eucharist. In the Eucharist He becomes present and He enters our body to live in us and to be that Radiant Light in us.

"This Light, this hope—what beautiful gifts!

"You came here to Betania with your weaknesses, your brokenness and the Lord wants to free you and to heal you. The Lord has received you here and Our Lady's presence here in Betania is a refuge for you, because she is your Mother. She waits here for many of her children to come and pray in this holy place.

"The Lord and His Mother have received you here in Betania, this holy place. It is like holy pilgrims on the way to Nazareth. This blessed land opens its arms to each one of you so that these moments with Jesus and His Mother will be special for you. This is a time of renewal for you. Thinking, believing and reaffirming the Life of Christ within you.

"I thank God for being able to share these moments of grace with you. Please pray that Our Lord will give me humility and patience and fear of God, not a God of chastisement, but a God so loving that we never offend Him.

"May Our Lady help each one of us to contemplate Her Son Jesus and to serve Him. Mary is inviting us, calling us to serve her Son.

"In all Our Lady's appearances she is calling us to serve one another, to love each other, and to reconstruct God's people. *Evangelize.* We are called to Evangelize. We are called to pray for our priests and pastors because they will be the ones to reeducate the 'People of God.' They are gifted with spiritual faculties and should be generous with these gifts and go forth into the vineyard to ease the pain and burdens of all our neighbors."

At Mass on the Feast of the Annunciation Father Vincent Von Euw blessed the several hundred crucifixes that we had brought with us. Before we left Maria Esperanza's house in Betania, she prayed over the crucifixes and gave one to each of us with the instruction to go back home and be "ambassadors of reconciliation."

2 Corinthians 5:11-21 (The Ministry of Reconciliation)

"Therefore, since we know the fear of the Lord, we try to persuade others; but we are clearly apparent to God, and I hope we are also apparent to your consciousness.

"We are not commending ourselves to you again but giving you an opportunity to boast of us, so that you may have something to say to those who boast of external appearance rather than of the heart. For if we are out of our minds, it is for God; if we are rational it is for you. For the love of Christ impels us, once we have come to the conviction that one died for all; therefore, all have died. He indeed died for all, so that those who live might no longer live for themselves but for Him who for their sake died and was raised.

"Consequently, from now on we regard no one according to the flesh; know him so no longer. Even if we once knew Christ according to the flesh, yet now we know Him so no longer.

"So whoever is in Christ is a new creation: the old things have passed away; behold, new things have come. And all this is from God, who has reconciled us to Himself through Christ and given us the ministry of reconciliation, namely, God was reconciling the world to Himself in Christ, not counting their trespasses against them and entrusting to us the message of reconciliation. So we are ambassadors for Christ, as if God were appealing through us. We implore you on behalf of Christ, be reconciled to God. For our sake He made Him to be sin who did not know sin, so that we might become the righteousness of God in Him."

Mary, Virgin and Mother of Reconciliation of All People, is calling everyone to be reconciled with God, to be reconciled within themselves, to be reconciled with family, friends, enemies and all people. Be "ambassadors of reconciliation."

Miracle of the Roses

At times the Eucharist has mysteriously appeared on Maria's tongue and recently, in a mystical way a bud, then a rose, has appeared on Maria Esperanza's chest. Before leaving Maria asked me how many pilgrims were in the group and she brought back three rose petals and proceeded to divide them into thirty-four pieces so that each one of us would have a "special" remembrance of our visit with her. Maria shared with me that many healings had taken place through the miraculous roses.

Chapter 8

Miracle
Of The
Eucharist

8

The Miracle
of the Eucharist

Our last day of the pilgrimage was spent visiting with Bishop Pio Bello Ricardo, the Bishop of Los Teques. Although his schedule was a busy one, he agreed to see us at his residence.

A conversation with Bishop Pio Bello Ricardo:

My name is Bishop Pio Bello Ricardo and I am the Bishop of Los Teques, which is the diocese where Betania is located. My name, Pio Bello, means holy and beautiful. Before we begin our little talk I don't know how holy I am and my English is anything but beautiful.

As the Bishop of Los Teques it is an honor for me to welcome you here and I particularly welcome those from the Boston area. It was my pleasure to have visited Boston about seven years ago.

I am happy that you have already been to Betania and spent a few days there. Our Lady has visited us in Betania. It is a sign of the times that Our Blessed Mother is visiting the Church. She is evangelizing the Church today.

We have the honor of being visited by Our Lady in Betania and also experiencing the "Miracle of the Eucharist." The Blood of Christ appeared on the Eucharist in Betania. I believe this miracle has only happened about twelve times.

The "Miracle of the Eucharist" took place in Betania on the Feast of the Immaculate Conception, December 8th, 1991.

Father Otty, a priest from Colombia and the Chaplain for Betania, was celebrating Mass for the vigil of the Feast of the Immaculate Conception. It was a midnight Mass. At the time of the Consecration about fifteen thousand people present saw a bright, rose light over the Host. There were several people on the altar, but none of them was aware of the bright ball of radiant rose light. At the time of Communion Fr. Otty broke the Host in half and broke off a small particle to put into the chalice. He had difficulty believing what he saw happening to the remaining part of the Host. It had begun to Bleed. It was truly the Body and Blood of Christ.

For three days the Blood on the Host was fluid, and then it began to dry up. Another small miracle is that the Blood didn't seep through the wafer thin Host. The opposite side of the Host shows no sign whatsoever of Blood.

The Blood on the Host is not a very large spot. The importance of the miracle is that it is a sign. Miracles are signs. The importance is not in the miracle itself, but in the sign. It is a sign that Our Lord is truly present in the Eucharist. In the miracles of the Bible it is not the miracle, but the sign—the sign of our Lord's mercy and love for His Children.

The "Miracle of the Eucharist" has been examined in laboratories and it is human blood, however we know that we cannot say that this is the Blood of Christ in heaven. The characteristics of the glorified Body of Christ in heaven is different than the Body of Christ before the Resurrection. St. Paul says, "The Body of Christ after the Resurrection is a spiritual body."

Again, it is a sign. It is a sign of the Transubstantiation and that is what is important for us today. God is trying to manifest to us that our faith in the consecrated Host as the Body and Blood of Christ is authentic.

I intend to construct a special altar in the Cathedral of my diocese of Los Teques for this "Miracle of the Eucharist."

Presently, the "Miracle of the Eucharist" is in the bishop's residence. It is my residence but I prefer to live here at this shrine and be with the Sisters of St. Joseph.

Bishop Pio Bello Ricardo rode with us to the Bishop's residence, where he gave us Benediction using the "Miracle Host." Each person on the pilgrimage was allowed to hold the container with the Host and to kiss it. Without any question it was the highlight of the pilgrimage for everyone.

Some said, "My life will never be the same. Never will I be able to receive Communion the same as

I have in the past." Others have said, "I have received many graces in my life, but never anything like this." And "How will I ever be able to thank God for this gift?"

Grotto in Betania

The "Miracle of the Eucharist" -
December 8th, 1991
Betania, Venezuela

Our Lady, Queen of Reconciliation
of All People

*The "Blue Butterfly" at the Medugorje Messengers Grotto
in Framingham, Massachusetts*

*Bishop Pío Bello
Ricardo of Los Teques,
Miranda, Venezuela,
and Reverend Vincent
Von Euw, Dorchester,
Massachusetts*

*Maria Esperanza in
Prayer - "White Smoke"
Sister Margaret
Catherine Sims, CSJ,
Reverend Vincent
Von Euw*

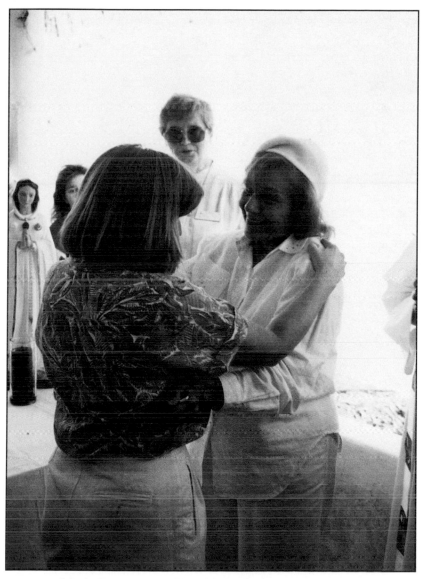

Maria Esperanza de Bianchini greeting a pilgrim from
Boston, Massachusetts

Pilgrims relaxing in Betania

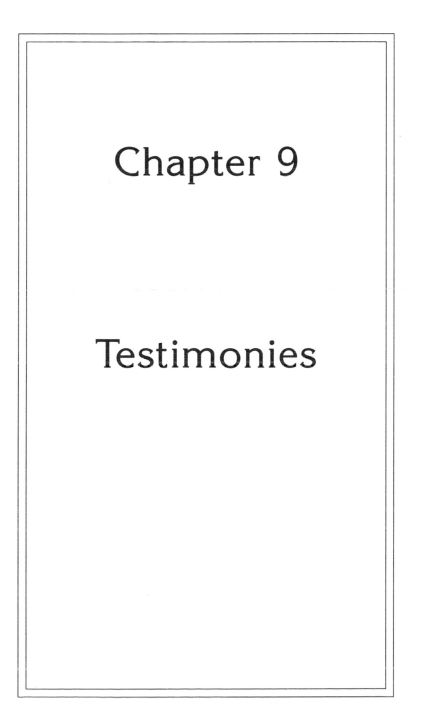

Chapter 9

Testimonies

9

Testimonies

It is important to prepare for a pilgrimage or a religious experience by praying and meditating a few weeks before. Having done this, I received a sense of peace and calmness going to Betania.

While in Betania, I had five incredible experiences. The first took place at Midnight Mass, the Mass of the Annunication on March 25th. There was such an overwhelming sense of belonging, as though the whole world was right there with me. Even though people were poor, they were so beautifully simple and we were all there to share the Eucharist and to give honor to Our Lady. Since the sermon was in Spanish, I prayed, reflected, and gazed at Maria Esperanza; she soon became my sermon. Her eyes were expressive. As the Bishop spoke, she smiled, nodded in agreement, and placed her hands on her heart. She clasped her husband's hand and looked at the Bishop with such reverence. This was truly beautiful!

After Mass, all through the night the pilgrims sang and clapped hands in joyful spirit. Different light phenomena were seen in the sky. As the moon glowed brightly through tall trees, it created an image for me of three separate beings, two adults and one little one. This signified the Holy Family to me. Soon a single image emerged, that of a woman with a head of a monstrance with rays. The image made no sense at the time, but when reflecting back home in Tampa, I realized the gift I had received that night in Betania. We have Adoration of the Blessed Sacrament for priests and religious in the chapel next to my office and the monstrance is very unusual. Our Lady is the stem section of the monstrance with its rays. We pray for priests, religious, the Church, and for an increase in vocations during the nine hours of adoration. That night in Betania, Our Lady showed me that she is pleased with our intentions and that she wants us to continue.

The third experience occurred at Maria Esperanza's home after a private Mass. She is such a holy person. I have seen other visionaries, but Maria's holiness, simplicity, and humility were so overwhelming. You could feel her "Christness" and her "Maryness." I knew that she had the gift to read one's soul, and I thought, "Wouldn't it be nice if she read my soul." As I approached her to receive my white plastic crucifix, my heart was racing. It calmed down as I got closer to Maria. She was looking at me and through me. I looked into her eyes and they turned to crystal. As her hand touched my face, I felt myself falling to the ground, resting in the Spirit, resting in the love of God. While I was on the floor, someone kissed me. I thought it was Maria because she was helping me up. However, looking back at the video that was taken, no one was close to my face as I lay on the ground. Our Lady gave me a sign that day.

I believe it was Our Lady who kissed me to let me know that the Lord was pleased with me and what I was doing for His Mother. Maria had read into my soul. I *was given* my answer.

My fourth experience occurred the evening before we left Venezuela. As Father Vincent celebrated Mass, I think everyone in our group shared the same love and desire for God. We were given a special, beautiful gift from Maria Esperanza - rose petals that mysteriously came forth from her heart, truly a gift from heaven. As I approached the altar to pick out my precious rose petal, I remember wanting one in the shape of a tear drop. There was one waiting for me! This was another affirmation because I have a great devotion to Our Lady, Rosa Mystica. Her red rose is a symbol of sacrifice and expiation for sins committed by priests and religious. And this is what I pray for — the expiation of their sins. I will continue to do so.

While viewing and adoring the "Eucharistic Miracle," I remember thinking that God will do anything to help strengthen our faith. I've never doubted the true presence of Jesus in the Eucharist, but some do, even priests. Great is the Lord's mercy and love for His people! As I knelt down to kiss the Host in the lunet, I experienced such sadness. Looking at the drop of Blood, I cried as I thought of Christ's suffering. He suffered so much! He loves us so much!

> Sister Carol Vinci
> Medugorje Messengers, Tampa, Florida

As I look back and reflect on my pilgrimage to Betania, I know that I was given special gifts, graces and blessings. They still keep coming! The miracle of the sun, the "blue butterfly," the bright light were all such special gifts. What a blessing it was to share in the celebration of the Eucharist on the Feast of the Annunciation with thousands of people I didn't know, but who were like one big, loving, and caring family all in love with Jesus and His Mother, Mary. What an incredible experience! I shall never forget it.

I shall always treasure the memory of the Mass celebrated at Maria Esperanza's home. My crucifix and the rose petal, gifts from Maria, are so dear to me. I went to Father Vincent for the sacrament of Reconciliation and I received a feeling of peace and love that seems to increase daily.

The "Eucharistic Miracle" has affected me the most. I have always believed that at the time of Consecration the bread and wine truly become the Body and Blood of Christ. I know that the accidents, (the taste, look, smell, and touch of the bread and wine) remain the same. Humbly He keeps coming to us because of His great love and mercy. His love and mercy for all people are beyond human comprehension. Jesus says in Scripture that He would continue to nourish us and that He would never leave us. My head believed this truth and in Medugorje my heart felt this truth. But now, in Betania, my whole being to its very depths could feel and experience Jesus' presence. My whole being felt the love and presence of Jesus.

As I knelt and looked at the drop of Blood on the Host, I sobbed unashamedly. I was looking at my Savior, my Redeemer, my Friend, Jesus for the first time in my life. I felt as if He had died on the cross for me and not for the billions of nameless people. He died for ME. I cannot put into words that beautiful feeling that flooded over me and still fills me every time I receive my Lord or gaze upon Him in the Blessed Sacrament. He is alive! He is real! He is present to me now! Praise be to Jesus Christ forever and ever! AMEN!

Susan Litchfield
Sturbridge, Massachusetts

Another pilgrim shared that he went on the pilgrimage to Betania when he heard that Our Lady was appearing under the title of Mary, Virgin and Mother of Reconciliation of All People. His wife had died in 1988 and in 1991 his son had been killed in an automobile accident. He would have to face the man who killed his son when the case came to trial and he wanted to have forgiveness in his heart instead of anger.

In Betania during the sacrament of Reconciliation Kevin realized he needed to forgive God for allowing his wife and son to be taken away from him in such a short period of time. Truly, Mary, Virgin and Mother of Reconciliation worked powerfully in his life during his brief stay in Betania.

Maria Esperanza de Bianchini radiates the love of

Mary, our Mother. Another one of our pilgrims shared her experience of this love. Avis came to know Jesus when she was sixteen and soon after was accepted into the Catholic Church. Her relationship with God is very important to her and through the years, Centering Prayer has kept her at peace and close to the Lord.

When Avis heard about the pilgrimage to Betania she was interested but had already signed up for a retreat on Centering Prayer. The priest giving the retreat broke his ankle forcing a cancellation which left her free to come with us to Betania.

There were many "special" experiences during the retreat. However, the Mass at Maria's house and the blessing afterwards were very important to Avis. She drew near to Maria and felt the visionary's gaze. She felt her own mother was looking at her and showering her with love, a love that she had never been able to give Avis when she was alive. It was a healing and blessed moment. Maria also had a word of knowledge for Avis telling her that Our Lady and her Son would appear to her three times.

Maria had a parting message for Avis, "You will receive an inner light - let that light guide you."

Chapter 10

Bethany

10

Bethany

The word Betania means "Bethany" in English and "Betania" can be found several times in Scripture. Bethany, a little village near Jerusalem, was also the home of Martha, Mary and their brother Lazarus. It was a favorite spot of Jesus and His apostles, where they would go for rest and relaxation among friends. It is quite appropriate that Our Lady's place of prayer in Venezuela should be called Betania. In the Gospel of Saint John we have the description of the raising of Lazarus at Bethany. Bethany was the place where Our Lord raised Lazarus from the dead, the place where He gave us the command to forgive one another, to be reconciled with each other, to "free" others.

Gospel of Saint John, Chapter XI (Verse 17-44)

When Jesus arrived, He found that Lazarus had already been in the tomb four days. Now Bethany was near Jerusalem, only about two miles away. And many of the Jews had come to Martha and Mary to comfort them about their brother. When Martha heard that Jesus was coming, she went to meet Him; but Mary sat at home. Martha said to Jesus, "Lord, if You had been here, my brother would not have died. But even now I know that whatever You ask of God, God will give You." Jesus said to her, "Your brother will rise." Martha said to Jesus, "I know he will rise in the resurrection on the last day." Jesus told her, "I am the Resurrection and the Life; whoever believes in Me, even if he dies, will live, and everyone who lives and believes in Me will never die. Do you believe this?" She said to Him, "Yes, Lord. I have come to believe that You are the Messiah, the Son of God, the One who is coming into the world.

When she said this she went and called her sister Mary secretly, saying, "The Teacher is here and is asking for you." As soon as she heard this, she rose quickly and went to Him. For Jesus had not yet come into the village, but was still where Martha and Mary had met Him. So when the Jews who were with her in the house comforting her saw Mary get up quickly and go out, they followed her, presuming that she was going to the tomb to weep there.

When Mary came to where Jesus was and saw Him, she fell at His feet and said to Him, "Lord, if You had been here, my brother would not have died." When Jesus saw her weeping and the Jews who had come with her weeping, He became perturbed and deeply troubled, and said, "Where have you laid him?" They said to Him, "Sir, come and see." And Jesus wept. So the Jews said, "See how He loved him." But some of them said, "Could not the One who opened the eyes of the blind man have done something so that this man would not have died?"

So Jesus, perturbed again, came to the tomb. It was a cave, and a stone lay across it. Jesus said, "Take away the stone." Martha the dead man's sister, said to Him, "Lord, by now there will be a stench; he has been dead for four days." Jesus said to her, "Did I not tell you that if you believe you will see the glory of God?" So they took away the stone. And Jesus raised His eyes and said, "Father, I thank you for hearing Me. I know that You always hear Me; but because of the crowd here I have said this, that they may believe that You sent Me." And when He had said this, He cried out in a loud voice, 'Lazarus, come out!' The dead man came out, tied hand and foot with burial bands, and his face wrapped in a cloth. So Jesus said to them, "UNTIE HIM AND LET HIM GO FREE."

I believe this passage from John describes Bethany in the past and what Bethany should mean in our lives today. Jesus prayed to the Father, thanking Him and praising Him for what He was about to do. "Father, I know that You hear Me." It is so important for us to know that our loving Father is listening to us and wants us to bring our cares to Him. He is waiting, listening to all His children.

Jesus called Lazarus to "come out." He called him to come out of the darkness into the light. He called him out of the stench; we certainly could say he was in a "stinking situation." "Lazarus, come out!" It is interesting to note that Scripture says, "The *dead* man came out." "Untie him and let him go free."

At Bethany, Jesus called forth Lazarus from the dead to life, but then turned to his relatives and friends and said, "Untie him, let him go free." Jesus is telling us to remove the bindings of rejection, unforgiveness, anger, hatred and let the Lord's peace, mercy and love flow. Be reconciled! Free one another! At Bethany in Venezuela, "the promised land," Mary, Virgin and Mother of Reconciliation of All People is asking us to give Her Son's life, "new life," to brothers and sisters, to bring the light of Christ into the darkness of sadness, depression, sickness, loneliness, and rejection. Remove the bindings and shackles.

Betania is a place of peace, comfort and love. Our Mother, Mary, is calling us to that peace, that true peace, which can only come through forgiveness and reconciliation. Forgive! Reconcile!

Prayer for Forgiveness

Forgive me my sins, Oh Lord, forgive me my sins; the sins of my youth, the sins of my age, the sins of my soul, the sins of my body; my idleness, my serious voluntary sins; the sins I know, the sins I do not know; the sins I have concealed so long, and which are now hidden from my memory. I am truly sorry for every sin, mortal or venial, for all the sins of my childhood up to this present moment. I know my sins have wounded your Sacred Heart. Oh my Savior, let me be freed from the bonds of evil through the most bitter Passion of my Redeemer. Oh my Jesus, forget and forgive what I have been and bless me this day.

Mary, Virgin and Mother of Reconciliation of All People intercede for me and for all my loved ones. Bring them to the foot of your Son so that we may be reconciled with Him and with each other.

Amen.

Chapter 11

Pastoral Letter

11

PASTORAL LETTER

written by

BISHOP PIO BELLO

(Bishop of Los Teques - November 21, 1987)

This Marian Year which we are celebrating by happy initiative of our Blessed Father John Paul II is an appropriate time to issue the present Pastoral Instruction on the apparitions of our Blessed Virgin Mary in Finca Betania.

Pio Bello Ricardo
Bishop of Los Teques

Los Teques, November 21, 1987

PASTORAL INSTRUCTION ON THE APPARITIONS OF THE BLESSED VIRGIN IN THE LAND OF BETANIA

Betania is an agricultural area which is located twelve kilometers from Cua, the parish of Our Lady of the Rosary of this diocese of Los Teques, a district in the vicinity of the State of Miranda, on the border left of the highway that joins that town of Los Valles del Tuy with San Casimiro in the state of Aragua.

In this spot, near the old and modest house on the property, there rises a hill from which descends a stream. At the foot of the hill it forms a little cascade. From this, luxuriant vegetation grows like a vegetable tunnel, which ascends along the course of the stream. There is where the apparitions have taken place.

The first apparition occurred March 25, 1976 (Feast of the Annunciation of the Lord). The only one to see Mary that day was Senora Maria Esperanza Medrano de Bianchini. Other people's relatives and friends (some eighty), who accompanied her that day, perceived only luminous phenomena and gyrations or movements of the sun. The same person saw the apparition again several times at the same site during the year indicated and in the two years following.

Besides her there are very few people who have declared seeing the apparition during that period, although they have testified to having perceived other phenomena as already noted: mist covering the mountain, brilliant light that reddened it, a profusion of flowers (non-existing there) which covered it, singing from an invisible choir, a play of lights, movement of the sun, etc.

From the time the first apparition was seen, centered in Betania, there was a movement of piety and religious formation promoted and directed by Senora Bianchini. There, people are reunited, especially at the end of the week on Marian feast days, to offer prayers and to reflect.

The Bishop of the diocese at that time, Msgr. Juan Jose Bernal, permitted some liturgical celebrations there. He himself administered the sacraments, especially in favor of the peasants and the neighboring houses. At the time, no formal ecclesiastical investigation was made regarding the happenings.

This situation, restricted to a relatively small number of participants, changed in the year 1984.

On Sunday, March 25, 1984, a group of approximately one hundred and fifty people met in Betania invited there for the celebration of a Mass at noon. Once the liturgy was celebrated in the old "trapiche" (some sort of building), those present dispersed throughout the house to take some refreshment and to rest.

Meanwhile, some youths and children were playing near the waterfall. Surprisingly, they saw the most Holy Virgin appearing over and behind it. It was very brief and afterward, they ran to relay the news to those who were together about one hundred and fifty meters away. They all hastened to the site of the apparition. There they were commenting on what had happened when the Virgin appeared again, being seen by all present. During that afternoon there occurred seven apparitions which lasted from five to ten minutes, except the last at nightfall, which lasted approximately one-half hour.

Naturally, the news of these events was spread among relatives and friends of those present. This produced a flood of visitors to the place, especially at the end of the week. The apparitions continued taking place with noticeable chronology, although generally on Saturdays and Sundays, and on days of Marian celebration. They were especially numerous during the years 1984 and 1985, more spread out during the years 1986 and 1987.

I-1. Ecclesiastical Investigation

The same week beginning with Sunday the twenty-fifth of March in 1984, there came to the diocesan curia the first witnesses who, spontaneously, wished to present to me their oral testimony of what happened and to give a written declaration.

I received them and questioned them kindly and openly, although as is normal for one having theological and psychological training and a knowledge of the history of the Church, having an interior attitude of doubt and scepticism. Therefore, given the quality of information and the data they were relating, I judged that the subject should be investigated seriously. As a matter of fact, I organized the convocation of protagonists and witnesses, no simple task, given the fact that the great majority resided in scattered, diverse cities outside the jurisdiction of the diocese.

I decided to personally conduct the investigation.

This permitted me to line up efficaciously my personal agenda with that of the possible witnesses, something that would, with great difficulty, have been possible if I had committed this task to a commission, given the number and dispersion of those testifying and the prolongation of the phenomena.

This option, as is obvious, obliged me to dedicate very much time to this subject, some four hundred to five hundred hours; but it has permitted me to interview with calm, approximately two hundred protagonists, and to gather, study and file three hundred and eighty-one written declarations. The majority of these were given during the course of the interviews. Considering that some of these testimonies were drawn up collectively, the number of people who confirm those declarations is four hundred and ninety. During this process, I abided by the criteria already classified in the Church, for the examination of this type of phenomena. I was preoccupied, above all, to determine the credibility of the witnesses; their background as people and as Christians, their sincerity, their mental state, their capacity for criteria, their critical sense, and their emotional equilibrium.

That credibility established, I tried to discern up to what point that might have been influenced by individual or collective suggestion.

I examined the spiritual effects or purely psychological effects produced in the people, such as the conduct of the groups that frequent the sight of the apparitions and especially the characteristics of the groups that, apart from them, have been forming themselves in a way of a movement of spirituality.

During my "ad limina" visit to Rome in September of 1984, I was received into the Sacred Congregation for the Doctrine of Faith. I deposited there a provisional report on the events and I was given a document for private use, worked out for said Congregation in 1978, with norms about the process that has to be followed to judge presumed apparitions or revelations. With satisfaction, I verified that the investigation, which up to that moment had been made, conformed to the criteria and proceedings which are indicated in that document and which, since then, have constituted my work guide.

I-2. Characteristics of the Apparitions

a. Identification

In other apparitions of the most Holy Virgin, Her figure could be identified by how much was presented in the same form with the same features and dress, which gave rise afterwards to her representation by means of images or paintings.

In the present case, the apparitions have been presented in various forms, through which the description, also varied, is made by observers according to the resemblance to known Marian titles, the most frequent descriptions being, "like the Virgin of Lourdes" (by the white dress and a blue sash, although they show that the arms are extended, a sign of greeting or welcome, and that the veil permits the hair to be seen, or also "like the Miraculous Virgin" possibly by the position of the arms and by the rays of light that come from the hands).

Although these are the most useful descriptions, there are also others, corresponding to the various Marian titles. The same concerned people have interpreted this circumstance as a teaching of the most Holy Virgin, who has wished to tell in detail that the titles are accessories with respect to her who is unique.

Already from the first apparition the most Holy Virgin presented Herself as "Reconciler of People", and this is the title or name by which she is recognized and venerated in this place.

b. Messages

There are very few people who claim to have held any verbal communication with the most Holy Virgin and to have received from her any instruction, message or counsel. Generally, they state in interrogations or in written testimonies that they have only seen and invoked her.

With regard to the content of the communications that bear witness to the ones that they have received during the apparitions, I point out the following factors:

  -Renewal of faith, as especially urgent in a world in which so many deny God and cast off the

117

supernatural, or practically dispense with God and the supernatural in their life.

-Deepening of faith, through reading and reflection on the Word of God in Sacred Scripture.

-Conversion from sin, and a full Christian life.

-Apostolic commitment is a consequence of that renewed, deepened and lively faith.

-A call to prayer, as a communication with God, and finally for the Church, for priests, for vocation, for the conversion of sinners, for peace in the world, for the imminent dangers that threaten humanity

-Frequent reception of the sacraments, especially reconciliation and the Eucharist.

-Solidarity, called to charity, especially with those most in need, the poor, those living on the fringes of society, the sick; persistence in brotherly tolerance, and the sense of each one sharing what he has with the rest.

In other cases the apparitions have been seen by a privileged few. In this situation, the number of witnesses is numerous, from the 25th of March 1984. That specific day one hundred people saw the seven apparitions: at least one hundred and eight gave testimony the same day with their signatures.

From that day witnesses were multiplying. With the exception of the day immediately before the one indicated, the norm has been that of a group of people present with only a few of them seeing the apparitions. Also it has been characteristic that those who on some occasion may have seen the apparition, on other occasions they have not had that privilege. Leaving the oral or written testimonies received, and the data obtained, and bearing in mind that the witnesses are scattered throughout different cities, with difficulty to locate them and to make an appointment with them, I assume that, up to now, from five hundred to a thousand people have seen the apparition.

c. Quality of the People

The usual thinking regarding apparitions of the most Holy Virgin is that those privileged, except very few, are of poor and uneducated conditions, and generally children or quite young people. In this case, there are at the same time, a number of economically well-situated people, of middle class, such as professional people of different university specialties; among them I mention medicine, psychiatry, psychology, engineering, and law. There are numerous students from different universities in Caracas.

d. Chronology

I pointed out before that the apparitions have not had an announced and predictable chronology or an established time period. Although generally they have taken place on Saturday, Sundays or on Marian liturgical feasts, they have also been taking place on unexpected week days.

e. Expectation

In relation to the foregoing characteristic, on numerous occasions, the hope seemed thwarted, for some of the people who had come to the place in the belief that some day on a Marian feast there would be apparitions, they, in fact, did not take place. On the other hand, on other occasions, a surprise apparition took place on March 25, 1984 in which the intention was simply to be present at an outdoor Mass on the property and to spend a day of enjoyment along the edge of a beautiful river in the pleasant rustic atmosphere. There are numerous statements to this a given fact, that for the witnesses a totally unexpected and unforeseen surprise took place. The instances of those who have gone out of idle curiosity, skeptically or even mockingly, or to enjoy a picnic at the end of the week and have seen the apparition which has transformed them, are not few.

f. Sense of Reality

There is a classical example in other apparitions where the visionaries fall into a psychological state of mystical or ecstatic trance. Apart from this, I tried to determine during the course of the visions, and upon studying the written testionies, whether in this case the loss of the sense of reality was present during the apparitions. I did not find such a phenomenon.

Of course, the visionaries are emotional but, with the exception of a few who have suffered weakness as a consequence of the emotion, they maintain the sense of reality during the course of the apparition. They speak of and compare among themselves the characteristics of what they are seeing. They also intend to explain them to one another for natural reasons (reflexes, tricks, suggestions, etc.) to be convinced that such reasons do not explain the reality of their vision. At most, some say that they have felt absorbed in thought during the apparition.

This characteristic facilitated my investigation on being able to dispense with the technical examination about the purely supernatural or psychological character of the state of ecstacy reducing my inquest to the determination of the credibility of the questioning and the value of the testimony.

g. Concomitant Phenomena

Along with all the apparitions there continued to be present phenomena which I indicated on giving an account of the first three years: the mist which appeared to hover over the trees on the hill, the intense light that inflamed it, the profusion of flowers which covered it, the intense fragrance of the flowers especially the roses, invisible choirs, the perfume of roses coming from the water, the play of lights and movement about the sun, etc.

These phenomena have been presented before or after the apparitions and even without their having happened.

h. General Ambiance

I have verified that the gatherings at Betania have taken place in an acceptable atmosphere from a religious point of view. There are serious occasions of long prayer, centered on the recitation of the rosary, the Way of the Cross and other current prayers, interspersed with sacred songs. The public is respectful and orderly except for the anticipated restlessness of the children. Cases have been presented of exaggerated emotionalism or hysterical reactions, but in general the atmosphere has been moderately balanced.

i. Effects

The effects have been good and some excellent. Those who are present receive a strong injection of faith and spirituality. People who never prayed, were praying the rosary. People who do not go to Church, now do so with regularity, go to confession and receive Communion. There have been notable conversions. It is consoling to hear confessions in this spot.

In all the interviews, I have noticed a disposition of

receptivity for what the church officially decides. All recognize having experienced an inner change in the feeling of drawing near to God and an impulse to a more Christian life.

I-3. Declaration and Judgement

From the beginning of my investigation, I noticed that it was not a case of fraud, collective suggestion or promotion of people or group interests but rather it dealt with a serious subject which had to be seriously investigated.

Relatively soon, along with my investigation, I became certain about the supernatural character of the phenomenon. I decided however to follow prudent practice and postpone all explicit statements about the phenomenon. With subsequent statements I would gauge the effects obtained and make critical pursuit of the religious movement produced by the events. I would then judge the opportune moment at hand for making public my judgement on these events.

Consequently, after having studied repeatedly the apparitions of the most Holy Virgin Mary in Betania, and having begged the Lord earnestly for spiritual discernment, I declare that in my judgement said apparitions are authentic and have a supernatural character.

I therefore approve, officially, that the site where the apparitions have occurred be considered as sacred, and that it be kept as a place for pilgrimages and as a place of prayer, reflection and worship in that liturgical acts may be performed, especially the celebration of the Mass and the administration of the sacraments of reconciliation and the Eucharist, always in accordance with the laws of the church and the norms of the diocese for pastoral unity.

I-4. Sense and Worth of this Statement

a. Competence

It is the responsibility of the diocesan Bishop to watch over and to intervene for judgement in every case of presumed apparitions or revelations that take place in the area of his diocese. This competence is derived from the hierarchical institution of the Church and has been expressly declared by the Sacred Congregation for the Doctrine of the Faith on indicating the norms that must be observed re: said subject.

b. Sense

As I shall tell in detail in a later paragraph, this declaration does not have magisterial value that would hold the contents of faith of public revelation, which God has given to the Church, in Sacred Scripture and Apostolic Tradition.

Their contents are of divine faith and on being explained or declared by the magisterium are of ecclesiastical faith: who does not admit his sins against the faith on rebelling against God and against the Church.

In the present case, it is a question of a religious deed which is admitted for human faith, founded on the testimony of witnesses; given the circumstances in my own testimony this last, as is obvious, especially authorized by the condition of pastoral guide that the Bishop has. The refusal to admit it does not constitute, however, a sin against the faith in that which every faithful member of the Church is obliged.

Who proceeds in such a manner will have to, nevertheless examine what his underlying motive is: whether it is prudence and a reasonable critical sense, or if it is a prejudiced attitude consequent to the scientific naturalistic mentality of those who do not admit except what is necessary for them with responsible evidence from mathematical calculations or laboratory experimentation. The skeptical attitude belongs to those who do not admit the possibility that God can communicate freely with his creatures and make invisible realities visible.

c. Pursuit

On making the present declaration I do not intend to affirm that all and each one of the apparitions occuring in Betania are authentic. I take for granted, as is customary to happen in similar circumstances, that here also there have been cases that are reduced to simple hallucination provoked by the expected, suggestion, emotionalism, and finally psychological unbalance.

In fact, in my investigation of the case of Betania, I too encountered a few happenings that inclined me to interpret as fantasies and which I have refused as valid testimony. I have judged since then that the presence of these events, on the one hand predictable, did not take away validity from the appreciable volume of numerous testimonies of those to which I concede credibility.

I-5. Public Revelations and Private Revelation

Faith is based on revelation. Throughout the years God wished to communicate with humanity by means of people privileged by Him for that purpose. In order that many truths thus taught be preserved, He raised up writers who, moved by divine inspiration, wrote Sacred Scripture. This is, therefore, the fountain from which we may drink the water that gushed from the spring of revelation.

At the end of this process of salvation God our Father sent us His Son Jesus Christ, the Word made flesh. In Him is perfected and culminated divine revelation.

Jesus Christ, in turn, entrusted to the apostles, as His authorized witnesses, the propagation of the total content of revelation. Their testimony was gathered in the books that form the New Testament, and preserved also by contemporaries in what is termed "Apostolic Tradition".

The contents of Sacred Scripture and Apostolic Tradition contain God's revelation, and we must accept them in virtue of the faith which the same God deserves. This theology expresses that these contents are "of divine faith."

On the other hand, Jesus Christ, on founding the Church, entrusted to the apostles and to their successors, the bishops, the authorized magisterium. On doing so, He commended to them the preservation and authorized interpretation of the contents of the revelation.

When the magisterium of the Church intervenes in the area of revelation in order to interpret it, to specify it, to explain it, etc., given that by the institution of Jesus Christ and the virtue of the Holy Spirit it enjoys the charism of magisterial authority. Its intervention must be accepted by every faithful Christian as content of faith, and its rejection is a sin against faith. The contents thus taught by magisterium, are known in theological terminology as "of Catholic" or "ecclesiastical" faith.

In Jesus Christ is culminated the divine revelation. With the words of the Second Vatican Council: "He, with His presence and manifestation, with His words and works, signs and miracles, above all with His death and glorious resurrection, with the sending of the Spirit of truth, He brings the fullness of revelation and confirms it with divine testimony...nor is there need to await any other public revelation before the glorious manifestation of Jesus Christ Our Lord." (Dv. n.4)

And with regard to the interpretation of revelation the Council agrees: "The Tradition and Scripture constitutes the sacred deposit of the Word of God confided to the Church. The office of authentically interpreting the Word of God, oral or written has been entrusted uniquely to the Magisterium of the Church, which exercises it in the name of Jesus Christ." (Du n.10).

The previous explanation does not imply the affirmation that dating from the death of the last apostle communication with God ceased or that after Jesus Christ revelations are impossible.

It would be a contradiction of the history of the Church in which, if cases of pseudo visionaries and false revelations abound, there are also many visionaries, apparitions and revelations which unite conditions that theological criticism requires as a sign of authenticity.

Yes, it implies, on the other hand, an important difference. The revelation contained in Sacred Scripture and Apostolic Tradition has, so to speak, an institutional character. Theology names it in such a sense "public" revelation. Whatever other revelation, although it may have as its end the spiritual welfare of the community, is designated "private" revelation.

What was properly entrusted by Jesus Christ to the Magisterium of the church was "public" revelation; and just as I indicated before when the Church intervenes re: it is obligatory for the faithful to obey and respect its decisions as "catholic" or "ecclesiastical" faith.

However, when the Church intervenes re: "private"

revelations, it does so for the time being, to determine the arrangement of the same with "public" revelation. Consequently, if it finds that "private" revelation contradicts "public" revelation, it declares it false, since God cannot contradict Himself. If it finds agreement between the two, it allows "private" revelations to be accepted. Generally the Church does not exceed this planning, that is, it does not proceed to declare positively the supernatural character of "private" revelations.

Nevertheless, although it is less frequent, the Church can also declare that, having encountered sufficient motives which accredit the supernatural character of a "private" revelation, it admits it as such. But, on doing so, it does not oblige the faithful to accept this statement as "of catholic or ecclesiastic" faith, but rather directs so that they may prudently admit it as human faith on the guarantee of investigation carried out and the guarantee of proper testimony of the ecclesiastical authority that issues the declaration. Such is the case of the present document.

Aside from this, if anyone wished to study the apparitions of Betania to form his personal criticism, he may have recourse to the documentation referring to the same. For that purpose I have taken the precaution to make photocopies of all statements in order to preserve as untouchable, the original ones which I consider to have no substitutions for their historic value.

I-6. Apparitions and Visions

The apparitions and visions can be pointed out as a constant of the history of salvation. Through these God grants the visionary the visible perception of realities invisible in themselves, but not in the concrete circumstances of time and place.

Visions or apparitions usually include some kind of message or teaching, generally oral. That is why, it is accustomed to be termed "private" revelation; although also it can be given this type of revelation without vision or apparition. From thence, an authentic vision or apparition, although it does not include any message, comes to be an implicit revelation on showing visibly the existence of the supernatural dimension, and on exhibiting visibly, invisible realities.

To admit or not to admit the possibility of visions and apparitions depends on the position that is taken before the possibility that they exist and can be picked up realities which transcend the material field of positive methods of investigation. Who denies the existence of such realities or the possibility of perceiving them, logically rejects the possibility of visions or apparitions and any type of revelation whatsoever.

Who believes in God, admits also that God can communicate with beings that he created. This possibility, of course, does not hold by itself that a concrete phenomenon constitutes a communication with God. It is necessary to purge critically each phenomenon in order to get the guarantee of what constitutes a supernatural deed. But the difficulty that exists to obtain that purification is not valid to reject, "a priori," its reality or to adopt an attitude systematically negative or skeptical.

There are numerous visions and apparitions described in Sacred Scripture, as many in the Old as in the New Testament. With respect to the supernatural authenticity of the same, we have the utmost guarantee, that divine inspiration confers, for the content of the sacred books and those that the divine magisterium of the Church offers us.

Equally numerous are those that the history of the church marks out, now from its origins in the patristic period, up to our own times. They form part of the charismatic dimension of the Church which is linked with its ministerial dimension; although to tell the truth, the ministerial dimension is a charism.

As the second Vatican Council expresses it in its constitution "Lumen Gentium," n. 12: "The Holy Spirit not only sanctifies and directs the people of God through the sacraments and ministrations and adorns it with its virtues, but also it distributes graces, including special ones, among the faithful of whatever condition, dispensing its gifts to each one as it wishes (1 Cor. 12, 11) with that which makes them able and ready to exercise the divine works and duties that may be useful for the renewal and greater edification of the Church." And over the extraordinary gifts it observes: "The judgement of its authenticity and reasonable exercise pertinent to those who have authority in the Church, to those upon whom it is incumbent above all not to stifle the Spirit, but to test it all and to retain what is good." (1Ts. d, 12y, 19, 21).

This text gives us the incentive to understand the meaning that visions, and apparitions, and private revelations have in the life of the Church. They pertain to its charismatic dimension; and they constitute a demonstration that Christ is present among us unto the consummation of the world (Mt. 28, 20), and that the Holy Spirit, soul of the Church, acts in it and gives it life.

In some cases, to enlighten and guide a definite person; in others, to promote a specific style of spirituality or a distinct form of pastoral action; in others, to actualize or renew evangelical lines that routine had rendered inoperable or inconsequence had termed marginal; in others, for the solution of a crisis or the acceptance of an historical challenge, as Pius XII points out in his encyclical "Mystici Corporis": "Join to this that Christ looks always with particular affection at His Immaculate Spouse, exiled in this world; and when He sees her in danger, whether by Himself, or by means of angels, or That One that we invoke as Help of Christians, and by heavenly intercessors, frees her from the waves of the storm, and calming the sea, consoles her with that peace that overcomes all feeling."

In the scheme of thought we can interpret the providential meaning that the apparitions of the most Holy Virgin have, that, from 1830 in the rue de

Bac, Paris, have constituted a series up to our own time. Typical of this century and a half has been the fact that man has believed in self-sufficiency, that his problems could be accomplished and solved by science, technology, social and political experimentation, human creativity, without recourse to God, and denying all intervention of transcendent and supernatural factors in human life. Now then the most Holy Virgin who "advanced" in the pilgrimage of faith, faithfully maintained union with her Son up to the cross (LG n. 56), and who preceded the Church being the "type of the Church in order of faith, of charity and of perfect union with Christ," (LG n. 63) and "as Mother of Christ is united in a particular way to the Church that the Lord established as His Body" (Juan Pablo II, "Redemptoris Mater", n 6), and she does not cease to be Star of the Sea for all those who follow the way of faith." (ibid 6).

We may thus think that God has wished that Mary our Mother in faith, who kept faithfully the teaching of the divine mysteries (Le 2, 19y 21), and whose visit to Elizabeth constituted the first spread of Christ's mystery (le 1, 39-45), visit the church in these last times as evangelizer in a period of crisis of faith.

I-7. Reconciler of People

On appearing, the most Holy Virgin at Betania presented herself as "Reconciler of People." I point out in this paragraph hints in order to understand what this title means theologically.

The most Holy Virgin, her person, her prerogatives, her activity, her essentially Christ-centeredness have meaning in Christ and for Christ. Jesus Christ is our only Redeemer and Mediator, as Saint Paul categorically declares: "There is only one God, and also only one mediator between God and Men, Christ Jesus, a man also, who delivered Himself as a ransom for all." (1 Tm. 2, 5-6). Nevertheless, "the unique mediation of the Redeemer does not exclude, but rather stirs up in creatures, different kinds of cooperation shared from the unique fountain." (LG n. 62).

John Paul II applied this doctrine to the most Holy Virgin: "The teaching of Vatican Council II presents the truth on the mediation of Mary as participation in this unique fountain which is the mediation of Christ Himself." ("Redemptoris Mater", n. 38).

As Mother of Christ Mary is mother of the Church which is the Body of Christ. "Conceiving Christ, giving birth to Him, nourishing Him, presenting Him in the temple to the Father, suffering with her Son when He was dying on the cross, she cooperated in an entirely singular way in the work of the Savior by her obedience, faith, hope and ardent charity, with the intention of restoring supernatural life to souls." (LG n. 61).

The Virgin is, then, cooperator with Christ in His work of redemption. And that cooperation did not end at the foot of the cross, but rather "given by her Son as Mother to the growing Church - behold your Mother...her Motherhood remains in the Church as maternal mediation." ("Redemptoris Mater" n. 40). "This Motherhood of Mary in the economy of grace endures unceasingly...until the perpetual consummation of all the elect." (LG n. 62)

On the other hand, redemption can, also, be proposed as reconciliation of all men with God and men among themselves. Compactly Saint Paul expresses it writing to the Romans and to the Ephesians: "We were reconciled with God by the death of His Son." (Rm. 5, 10) "He is our peace, He that of two people made one, tearing down the wall that separated them, enmity...to create in Himself, of the two, one single new man...making peace...giving in Himself death to hostility." (Ef. 2, 14-16)

Being the most Holy Virgin cooperator in the redemption, she must be logically considered as cooperator in reconciliation.

In this role, she is the one who receives and proclaims the title of "Reconciler" or "Mother of Reconciliation."

That this condition of cooperator in reconciliation does not remain circumscribed in the earthly life of Jesus, but rather is prolonged in the history of the Church, we may consider it implied in the passage in which St. Luke narrates the event of Pentecost.

The outpouring of the Holy Spirit takes place as a consequence of having realized the reconciliation of men with God, and produces the reconciliation of men with one another, symbolized by the breakdown of the barrier which impeded comprehension with the multiplicity of languages. (hch. 2, 5-12)

In those circumstances the Virgin is mentioned singularly cooperating with her prayer.

The cooperation is prolonged indefinitely. "This motherhood (mediator) of Mary, in the economy of grace, lasts forever...until the perpetual consummation of all the elect." (LG n.62).

If something has characterized humanity in this last century and a half it is guerilla warfare, violence, hatred among people and among social classes and nations, divisions of hearts and of deeds and wars. There have surged initiatives for peace and for union and there have been plans made for this purpose. But all the plans have been ineffective, because they have only touched the surface of human life. They do not go deep into hearts and souls where germinate as a result of original sin (the seed of hatred and division).

In the bosom of the Church has arisen the ecumenical movement which desires to restore the unity of all Christians in Christ. But this movement comes up against the walls raised during centuries of opposition.

And justly so. In this world and in this Church there appears the most Holy Virgin as Reconciler of People. She insists on the spirit of solidarity and mutual brotherly sharing. The title springs from theology on the cooperation of Mary in redemption-reconciliation, and the message holds much sense for the present day.

I-8. Conclusion

On concluding this Pastoral Instruction, I thank the Lord because He has granted to our diocese and to our country the privilege of the most Holy Virgin's visit. At this time in our Church history, symbolized by a new evangelization, it links us to the renewal and deepening of the faith and to the protection of that faith in a complete conversion in prayer and in apostolic commitment. In this divided world she must be presented as Reconciler of People.

The Lord wanted to grant us, by our Mother's visit, that outpouring of the Holy Spirit that He granted to Elizabeth when she visited her. And if on that occasion she proclaimed "from now on all generations will call me blessed, because the almighty has done marvels in me" (Lc. 1, 48-49), then through her intercession may be realized marvels in all the faithful who piously draw near to the place where she manifested her presence.

Given in Los Teques, Nov. 21, 1987 Pio Bello Ricardo, Bishop of Los Teques.

I-9. Opinion of Mariologist Rene Laurentin

Rev. Father Rene Laurentin, Mariologist recognized world wide as theologian and investigator, in his last work on the modern apparitions of the Virgin gives an account of those at Betania. After referring to the Pastoral Instruction of Monsignor Pio Bello Ricardo and citing the judgement issued about her, he says "This official recognition is a new act, since no apparition had obtained any such authentication since up to the middle of the century. This is explained because the Bishop, at once scientifically formed and endowed with discernment, could unite, without dissociation, the critical requirement and pastoral sense. As God's gardener, he has cultivated spiritual fruits from these apparitions. It has been for him and his people a fountain of well-being." (Rene Laurentin, Multiplication des apparitiones de la Vierge aujourd 'hui, Editorial Fayard, Paris, 1988; pag. 54).

Medugorje Messengers located in Framingham, Massachusetts is a non-profit organization dedicated to spreading Our Lady's messages. In Medugorje, Bosnia-Herzegovina, Our Lady calls us to Prayer, fasting, faith, conversion and to peace. In Betania, Venezuela we are called by Our Lady to forgive and to be reconciled with each other.

Books, videos and information pertaining to pilgrimages can be obtained by writing to:

Medugorje Messengers
P.O. Box 647
Framingham, Massachusetts 01701